HEAVEN'S THRONE GIFT

Heaven's Throne Gift

by

JAMES A. STEWART
Author-Missionary

Author of

Evangelism
Lordship of Christ
The Normal Christian Life
Hollywood Evangelism
Ecumenical Evangelism

etc. etc.

REVIVAL LITERATURE
1844 73rd Avenue, Philadelphia, Pa. 19126

Printed in the United States of America

by

THE CONTINENTAL PRESS, Philadelphia 6, Pennsylvania

43,577

DEDICATED

to

*the memory of Walter E. Weeks, whose devotion to
Christ was characterized by his fervent and practical
interest in foreign missionary work.*

Foreword

IT IS ONLY AFTER MUCH EXERCISE OF SOUL and deep humility before God that we have undertaken this study of the person and work of the Holy Spirit. Oftentimes we have asked ourselves if there are not enough books already written on this all-important subject to meet the need in evangelical circles around the world today. Actually, the only plea we can give for setting forth another book of this kind is that we have been guided to do so by the Divine Spirit Himself. For over thirty years we have been speaking to large groups of ministers at the home fronts and to lonely missionaries on the foreign mission fields on this sacred theme. During this time there has been much heart-searching and many hours spent at the Throne of Grace with the Word. During this time many hungry pastors, professors, Bible teachers, evangelists and missionaries have asked us again and again to tell them more about the ministry of the Holy Spirit. This book is set forth as an answer to these requests.

Almost all the weakness, both personal and corporate, in the Church of God today may be traced to an incomplete understanding of and recognition to the Holy

Spirit. To many saints He is known only as an influence, intermittent at best. They ascribe their new birth to Him, but know little or nothing about His controlling and sanctifying presence and power in their lives. Hence, Christian life to them has become a long weary struggle to attain to the ideal of Christ's example; and very many, sadly recognizing the difference between the ideal and the actual; between Christ's life and theirs, have settled down to the calm of despair. Interpreting the Word of God by their own experience, they have concluded that no higher type of life is possible for them in this world. It is with a desire of helping these dear believers that this book is set forth.

We firmly believe that most of the problems that confront the Pilgrim Church today would find their solution in a full recognition of the true place of the Holy Spirit as the divine Administrater of our affairs. All the vexing questions and problems concerning Christian unity, foreign missionary activity, the powerlessness of the Church at home and sufficient funds for carrying on the work of the Lord in the world, would be fully solved if the mind of the Spirit were sought and His will obeyed.

Again, many questions that trouble the believer in his own personal life regarding his daily walk and witness would be answered by a full recognition of the Paraclete.

We would humbly suggest that this is not an exhaustive book on the ministry of the Spirit. For example, we have not mentioned the miraculous gifts of the Spirit in the Body of Christ today. We have felt that this is a subject too vast to be dealt with adequately in one chapter, and so have reserved it for a book by itself.

It may be that some will doubt our wisdom in using

the term "Baptism" in relation to the power of the Spirit. We realize that a vast number of our friends stick strictly to the term "fulness" in referring to this subject. However, we have only followed our firm conviction on this matter. We believe, along with the early Puritans, as well as C. H. Spurgeon, R. A. Torrey, A. B. Simpson, Andrew Murray, A. C. Dixon, and "La Marechale," that the New Testament teaches a baptism of power for Christian service. We have not written from an argumentive or dogmatic viewpoint. The high and holy mystery of the Spirit's person and ministry demands our silent worship, and the recognition of His majesty claims our unconditional obedience. It is imperative to guard against uncharitable conclusions concerning other believers using terms different from our own.

William Romaine, one of the leaders of the great Evangelical Revival in the 18th Century wrote: "I am sure God the Holy Ghost is the best Writer; and I find Him the best Expositor upon His own writings." We earnestly plead with the reader that he read this book upon his knees in the quietness before God, with his Bible at hand. There can be no doubt that the divine Author of the Scriptures is the best Expositor, and that under His teaching the Bible is its own best commentary.

We once again thank our kind friends who have spread our messages around the world. We sincerely ask the united prayers of the saints of God for Heaven's richest blessing to rest upon the message of this book. Any portion or portions of it may be freely used for reprinting in any part of the world, for His glory.

As the late devoted William Pennefather of Mildmay, London, wrote in a pastoral letter to his people:

"We are hoping that very much prayer may ascend to God for the fresh anointing of the Holy Ghost. Surely it is *this* which is our great want. We have many faithful preachers, and many earnest laborers, and various instrumentalities for the benefit of those around us; but the 'fresh oil' from the sanctuary is too often lacking. 'O God, Thou art my God, early will I seek Thee; my heart and my flesh cry out for the LIVING God!'

"When God makes Himself manifest in creation, what a sense there is of fresh power! How vigor and vitality appear as springtime comes on! Do not we want a springtime in the Church of Christ? Alas! Alas! there are so many dead leaves of OLD PHRASES in prayer, and of old ceremonies in worship, that we can scarce find the living presence of the Divine Comforter.

"May God give us more of His own blessed anointing, and work for Him will NOT THEN be a toil."

I would like to express my deep appreciation to Miss Mary Henderson, Miss Lillian Elliott, and my own wife for their practical help in preparing the manuscript.

JAMES STEWART
SALZBURG, AUSTRIA.
JUNE, 1956

Contents

One

The Naming of the Spirit

"THE COMFORTER"—The patron, one that pleads and defends the cause of another."

"Our ADVOCATE, Who was to be, and has been, an Advocate for Christ against the world, and for His people, against all their enemies: and Who, as He was to reprove, and did reprove the world of sin, righteousness, and judgment, in favour of Christ, so He was to assist His people and plead their cause, and help them, in vindication of themselves before the princes of the earth, as He did; and who also was to act, and has acted the part of a Comforter to them, under all the hatred and violence they have met with from the world, by taking and applying the things of Christ to them."

John Gill

To Thee, O Comforter Divine,
For all Thy grace and power benign,
   Sing we Alleluia!

To Thee, whose faithful love had place
In God's great Convenant of Grace
   Sing we Alleluia!

To Thee, our Teacher and our Friend,
Our faithful Leader to the end,
   Sing we Alleluia!

To Thee, by Jesus Christ sent down,
Of all His gifts, the sum and crown,
   Sing we Alleluia!

To Thee, Who art with God the Son
And God the Father ever One,
   Sing we Alleluia!

J UST AS THE SON WAS GIVEN A NAME from all eternity, the name of His incarnation—Jesus (Matt. 1:21), so the Spirit was named for His temporary mission here upon earth. Just as we all like to sing with John Newton, "How sweet the Name of Jesus sounds," so we can rejoice in the name of the Eternal Spirit, that of *Paraclete*. This name was given to Him by the Lord Jesus when He prophesied of His advent.

Theologians have for centuries discussed at great issue the meaning of this precious name of Paraclete. In our Authorized Version the Greek word "Paraclete" (Parakletos) is translated "Comforter." John Wycliffe translates it as "Advocate." The word Paraclete comes from two Greek words meaning "alongside" and "I call." The metaphor is derived from a law court trial. A defendant is hard-pressed by the opposing barrister and, being unable to defend himself, espies across the court the familiar face of an influential friend, whom he beckons to him. His friend threads his way through the crowd until he stands beside him. From that moment on he is the Paraclete—standing beside, suggesting, enabling to withstand. Westcott says, "In defining this

3

word the sense of advocate, counsellor, one who pleads, convinces, convicts in a great controversy; who strengthens on the one hand and defends on the other, meeting formidable attacks, is alone adequate."

The Paraclete will comfort, strengthen and defend those purchased by the precious blood of Christ. It is only as we know the Person that we can fully interpret His name aright. In the Upper Room discourse we see the Holy Spirit as a Person Who teaches, reminds, testifies, comes, convinces, guides, speaks, prophesies, takes and brings. He is revealed, not only as a Person, but as a Divine Person:

1. Only a Divine Person could take the place of another Divine Person.

2. He that is able to teach the apostles all that is necessary for the execution of their ministry must know the "all things" of Christ.

3. He that is able to bring to the disciples' remembrance whatsoever Christ had said unto them must needs be God, because He must know their hearts and thoughts.

Many have thought, because of an unfortunate translation of our Lord's words in John 16:13: "He shall not speak of Himself," that possibly the Spirit was not on the same equality with the Father and with the Son. Weymouth's translation clarifies the true meaning of the verse: "He will not speak as Himself originating what He says, but all that He hears He will speak." This does not mean that the Holy Spirit does not speak of Himself. It simply means that He, in His position of humiliation and subordination in His temporary mission as Paraclete, would not speak on His own initiative or from His own authority. In other words, He does not utter different truth from that uttered by the Lord Jesus. There is no such thing as the Gospel according

4

to the Holy Spirit. The coming Paraclete would not teach a new body of truth. (We note that the expression used in John 16:13 is the same used by our Lord in John 14:10, "I do not speak on my own authority." Weymouth)

We see that, in their circumstances, the sorrowing disciples desperately needed one who could comfort and strengthen them, and champion their cause. Our Lord said to them, "I am going to request the Father that He will give you One Who will ever stand beside you in every hour of persecution, telling you how to answer (Matt. 10, 19-20); in every moment of temptation making you able to overcome (Acts 9:31); in all hours of prayer helping your infirmities (Romans 8:26); and in all the preaching of My holy Gospel, making you conscious that One is standing beside you whose words corroborate your own, so that while you speak to the outward ear, He will speak moment by moment to the heart" (Acts 10:44).

It is a common mistake to think that our Lord Jesus is more interested in our everyday affairs than is the Holy Spirit. We must never forget that the love of the Spirit is as true as that of the Son. The Psalmist says, "Thy Spirit is good" (Psalm 143:10). Paul cries to the Roman believers, "Now I beseech you, brethren, for the Lord Jesus Christ's sake, and *for the love of the Spirit,* that ye strive together with me in your prayers to God for me." (Romans 15:30). If the Divine Spirit sheds abroad in our hearts the love of God, (Romans 5:5) then surely He loves us deeply Himself.

Horatio Bonar is one of the few men who has entered into the secret of this vital truth. Speaking of this glorious love of the Spirit, he says, "The want of *stable peace,* of which so many complain, may arise from imperfect views of the Spirit's love: as if there was something in

5

the Spirit which repelled us, whatever there might be in Christ to attract us; as if the light which the Cross throws upon the love of the Spirit were not quite in harmony with that which it reveals of the love of Christ; as if the Spirit were not always as ready with *His* help as is the Son. True, our peace comes from the one work of the Substitute upon the Cross, from the blood of the one Sacrifice, from the sin-bearing of Him Who has "made peace by the blood of His cross"; but it is the Holy Spirit Who glorifies Christ to us and takes the scales from our eyes.

"If we, then, doubt His love, can we expect Him to reveal the Son in our hearts? Are we not thrusting Him away and hindering that view of the peace-making He alone can give? . . . . Perhaps the *want of faith*, which we often mourn over may arise from our not realizing the Spirit's love. 'Faith cometh by hearing and hearing by the Word of God.'" Yet it is the Holy Spirit Who shines upon the Word. It is He Who gives the seeing eye and the hearing ear. Under the pressure of unbelief, have we fled to Him and appealed to His love? "Lord, I believe, help Thou mine unbelief", may be as aptly a cry to the Spirit as to the Son of God. He helpeth our infirmities; and in the infirmity of our faith, He will most assuredly succour us. It is through Him that we become strong in faith, and He loves to impart the needed strength. Yet, in our dealings with Him regarding faith, let us remember that He does not operate in some mystical and miraculous way, as if imparting to us a new faculty called "faith"; but by taking of the things of Christ and showing them to us; so touching our faculties by His mighty yet invisible hand, that ere we are aware, these disordered souls of ours begin to work aright, and these dull eyes of ours begin to see what was all along before them, but what they had never perceived, "the excellency of the knowledge of Christ Jesus our Lord."

Into the blessed Name of "The Paraclete" we can write the answer to all our needs. The Spirit will see us right through to the "bitter end." This One, "called alongside to help," stands by us in the hour of sorrow. During World War I, a commanding officer of a southern district of England, came to a certain quiet little village, and requested the rector of the parish to break the news to a mother that five of her sons had been lost. The man of God went down on his knees with his wife and they prayed together: "O God, give us grace to break the news to our sister!" As the rector walked up the beautiful garden walk, suddenly the mother opened the door of the house, her hand clasped to her bosom. She cried out, "O Rector, Rector, which one, which, one, which one?" The rector sadly answered: "Not, 'which one,' all five, all five!"

With tears streaming down her face, the mother cried: "Oh Jesus! Oh Jesus! Oh, my wonderful Lord!" She had immediately received comfort. Then she invited the rector to come in, and she got down on her knees and gave God thanks for the gift of her sons and also for the perfect peace she had in her heart. That clergyman said that in all his life he had never known such wonderful peace caressing the heart of a dear child of God.

As we are writing this, we have just received a letter from our dear friend, Sidney Evans, on the death of his beloved wife and partner. For over fifty years Mrs. Evans (sister of Evan Roberts of the Welsh Revival), rendered faithful and fruitful service to her Saviour in the homeland, in Africa and in India. Mr. Evans writes, "The call to higher services was unexpected—it came through a second operation from which she never fully regained consciousness. Thus did Jesus answer His own prayer—'Father, I will that they whom Thou hast given

7

me, be with me where I am' (John 17:24)."

Fellow believer, you may be perplexed, you may be lonely, you may be in sorrow, you may be tempted, you may be at wits-end corner, but when you are filled with the Holy Spirit, He will be your Comforter and your Sufficiency, and He will meet every need of your heart.

The Spirit, however, is not limited to the ministry of comfort. The disciples had a greater need than comfort in face of the loss of their earthly Friend. They had a charge to keep. "And ye also shall bear witness because ye have been with Me from the beginning" (John 15:27). They were faced with an impossible task of preaching a crucified Jesus as the majestic Son of God, and God's glorious Redeemer. Who would believe that He Who died a felon's death on a Roman gibbet was Emmanuel! Thank God we are not sent to war at our own charges! Our Lord said, "But when the Paraclete is come, whom I will send unto you of the Father, even the Spirit of truth, which proceedeth from the Father, *He shall testify of Me.*" There is to be a testifying of the Spirit *in* the world, corresponding to our testifying *to* the world. The Holy Ghost stands by and corroborates our simple testimony. As R.S. Candlish has stated, "His testifying is an internal, subjective influence or operation in the world, to which our testifying is an external, objective address." It is the work of the Spirit to convict the world of its damning sin of Christ-rejection * (John

* As witnesses, we feel the constant need of beckoning to our Paraclete for help. How often we, as ministers of the Gospel, feel in the meetings a deadness and a heaviness which is impenetrable. We desperately lift our hearts in prayer, pleading the divine intervention of our Paraclete, and suddenly the heaviness disappears, the atmosphere is charged with His Divine Presence, our audience becomes suddenly alive, and we rejoice that from that moment the message and the meeting are no longer in our hands! Blessed Paraclete! Blessed promise! "When the Paraclete is come . . . . He will be a witness unto Me."

8

16:8). (What a tremendous issue and responsibility it is to witness for Christ! When you speak to men about their desperate need of a Saviour, and you deliver your own soul, whether they hear or not, they stand guilty before God.) The glorious promise to him who witnesses is: "But ye shall receive power, after that the Holy Ghost is come upon you; and ye shall be witnesses unto me" (Acts 1:8).

An old Brymbo miner, who was transformed during the Revival in Wales in 1859, said, "When I was a boy we dug out coal with chisels; after that came dynamite, and with this we mine a much bigger quantity of coal. Till this week I have seen nothing but chisel work in our churches, but now here is God's dynamite at work!" Only when we witness in the power of the Spirit can the Gospel be "the power (dynamite) of God unto salvation" (Rom. 1:16). With what drudgery we plan and scheme and work to bring men to Christ, all because we ignore the Spirit's ministry! There is too much chisel work in our churches to-day. Thus it is that the Paraclete meets our need for spiritual power in witnessing.

"The Spirit breathes upon the Word,
And brings the truth to sight."

9

Two

The Good News of Pentecost

"The Holy Spirit is pleased to open and reveal to the understanding of the believer the mysteries of the Person of Christ—that He is God-man, the brightness of His Father's glory, and the express image of His person, in whom dwelleth all the fulness of the Godhead personally; he being the Son of the living God dwelling personally in our nature, which He took hold of, and assumed into union with Himself; so that He is God dwelling personally in our nature, God and man united, the man 'Jehovah's fellow, the equal of the Lord of Hosts' (Zech. 13:7)."

Samuel Eyles Pierce

"The fund whereon the Holy Spirit would draw is the glory of Christ. This is the test of true ministry. Does it exalt Christ? That which does so exalt Him is of the Holy Ghost. That is not of the Spirit that overlooks Christ. This is the Spirit's wide field— Jesus' Person and work."   *Robert Govett*

"And I will pray the Father,
And He shall give you
Another Paraclete,
That He may abide with you forever;
Even the Spirit of Truth;
Whom the world cannot receive,
Because it seeth Him not,
Neither knoweth Him:
But ye know Him;
For He dwelleth with you,
And shall be in you." (John 14: 16-17)

"These things have I spoken unto you,
Being yet present with you.
But the Paraclete,
Which is the Holy Ghost,
Whom the Father will send in My Name,
He shall teach you all things,
And bring all things to your remembrance,
Whatsoever I have said unto you." (John 14: 25-26)

"When the Paraclete is come,
Whom I will send unto you from the Father,
Even the Spirit of Truth,
Which proceedeth from the Father,
He shall testify of Me:
And ye also shall testify,
Because ye have been with Me from the beginning." (John 15:26-27)

"It is expedient for you that I go away:
For if I go not away,
The Paraclete will not come unto you;
But if I depart, I will send Him unto you.
And when He is come,

12

He will reprove the world of sin,
And of righteousness
And of judgment:
Of sin, because they believe not on me;
Of righteousness, because I go to my Father,
And ye see me no more;
Of judgment, because the prince of this world is judged.
I have yet many things to say unto you,
But ye cannot bear them now.
Howbeit, when He, the Spirit of Truth is come,
He will guide you into all truth:
For He shall not speak from Himself;
But whatsoever He shall hear,
That shall He speak:
And He will show you things to come.
He shall glorify Me:
For He shall receive of Mine, and shall show it unto you.
All things that the Father hath are Mine:
Therefore said I, that He shall take of Mine,
And shall show it unto you." (John 16: 7-15)

THE ENTIRE LIFE OF A BELIEVER IN
Christ may be revolutionized by accepting in simple
faith the scriptural doctrine of the ministry of the Paraclete. I believe that in John, chapters fourteen, fifteen
and sixteen, we have the deepest and highest teaching
concerning the ministry of the Holy Spirit. The words of
our Lord concerning the Person and doctrine of the
Spirit should be read prayerfully and carefully day after
day on our knees, until the very glory of these precious
truths floods and fills our souls.

I make bold to say that no one can have a clear
conception of the person and ministry of the Spirit of
Pentecost, if he ignores the teaching set forth in these
chapters. Here are the real vital facts concerning His
blessed person and work. If I go to the Acts and the
Epistles and ignore these chapters, I will only have an
imperfect and incomplete view of the subject. Here
is a reservoir of Scripture doctrine. A preacher could
easily preach many sermons on one single utterance of
Christ as it fell from His gracious lips in the Upper
Room. These words were not spoken in cold technical
language to theologians, but from a tender, overflowing

15

heart to sorrowing disciples.

The Lord wanted to prepare His disciples for the future. He must make known to them His death on Calvary's Cross, and also the incarnation of the Holy Spirit. In the middle of His discourse, He drops, as it were, a bombshell in their midst, by announcing to them His departure. The disciples were startled, perplexed, even dazed, and they cried in effect: "Lord Jesus, we cannot live without Thee! As the ivy clings to the wall, we cling to Thee. Lord, Thou art our life! Lord, Thou must not go away! Lord, Thou canst not go away! Lord, we would be failures; Thou must not leave us; We cannot live without Thee!"

To these perplexed disciples the Lord Jesus gave the most wonderful news about the coming and the ministry of the Paraclete. He said in effect: "Yes, because I have told you I go away, sorrow has filled your hearts. Now do not let your hearts be troubled; do not let them be afraid. Listen! I have some wonderful news for you" (John 16:6 and 14:1).

I am sometimes sorry that I am a Scotsman. We Scots have a rough type of voice, and sometimes I wish we could speak more tenderly. When I am preaching the Gospel to the unconverted, I wish I could quote Matthew 11:28 in the way the Saviour must have said it. And I wish I could say these words, the words uttered in the Upper Room concerning the coming and ministry of the Holy Spirit, in the way Christ spoke them. While their hearts were filled with sorrow, His heart was filled with joy, because He knew the Holy Spirit and His gracious ministry. He knew the untold blessing that was to be the portion of the disciples, and so He said, "And I will pray the Father, and He shall give you another Comforter, that He may abide with you forever. I will not leave you comfortless; I will come to you."

Let us put ourselves in the place of these disciples. Suppose we had lost a loved one, say on the battlefield, as so many of us have. What we desire most today is to see that lovely face and hear that tender voice. The disciples were like that. They wanted no substitute; they wanted to see Christ alone with them, and to hear His voice. Yes! all the disciples wanted was the Lord Jesus Christ, Himself, and herein lies the significance of His words. He says that the coming of the Holy Spirit is to be as though He Himself were coming.

Our Lord did not say that He would request of the Father a Comforter. The key to His message was that the Father would send in His name ANOTHER Comforter. Why another? Because He Himself was the first Comforter, and The Holy Spirit would be the second Comforter. He would be another Person just like the Lord Jesus. As you know, there are two Greek words for "another:" HETEROS, meaning another of a different kind, from which we get our English word, Heterodoxy. Paul uses this word in his letter to the Galatians, when he says, "another Gospel" (Gal. 1:6). The other word for "another" is ALLOS, meaning another of the same kind or quality. Hallelujah! this is the word the Lord uses here! The word "another" does not connote one who is instead of someone else, but rather a second person who is in addition to the first. As one has said, "The absence of one is the presence of the other; or let me rather say, that there is no absence, no distance, no departure, no separation! Christ, Himself, is one with His Holy Spirit, and with Him, temples in the heart of His mystical body." Thus, our Lord makes the same even to be at once His coming, and His sending; and He speaks of the Spirit now, as His own Presence, and now as His Substitute during His absence. In other words, one of the vital truths of the Upper Room is

17

this, that in the Person of the Holy Spirit, the Lord Jesus, as the risen, exalted, glorified Redeemer would come to His disciples. Though henceforth they will not know Him "after the flesh," they will know Him in a more intimate, dynamic way (II Cor. 5).

"At that day, ye shall know that I am in my Father, and ye in Me, and I in you" (John 14:20). It is well to assert that the Spirit did not become Christ in the incarnation at Bethlehem; nor does the Redeemer become the Spirit at Pentecost. Moberley has expressed this mysterious truth in these words: "It is not for an instance that the disciples are to have the Presence of the Spirit instead of the Son, for to have the Spirit is to have the Son." The Holy Spirit does not supersede the work of Christ in the sense that Christ ceases to work, and the Spirit takes His place, but the work of Christ Himself is continued in the Spirit's work, under new conditions, both outward and inward.

The Holy Spirit should not be a stranger to any believer. No believer should feel strange in the presence of the Spirit, because He is another Christ. Does this seem blasphemous to you? I would point you to the incident in the early verses of this chapter. Philip had requested, "Lord, show us the Father, and it sufficeth us." Jesus saith unto him, "Have I been so long time with you, and yet hast thou not known me, Philip? He that hath seen me, hath seen the Father" (John 14:8-9). "Philip, gaze upon Me. Philip, you are now looking at the Father!" Yes, Christ was the brightness of God's glory and the effulgence of His Person (Heb. 1:3). "God was in Christ . . ." (II Cor. 5:19). Just as the Son came to reveal and glorify the Father, so the Holy Spirit is come to reveal and glorify the Son. He is thus another Paraclete; another Lord Jesus. The fulness of Pentecost is therefore the fulness of the risen life of Christ, enjoyed

18

by His disciples. The blessing of Pentecost is the communication of the life of the Redeemer to the believers by the Spirit. "Because I live, ye shall live also" (John 14:19).

All that the Lord Jesus Christ had been to His disciples, the Spirit, as another Paraclete, would be. The companionship would be the same in content, but the mode would be inward, not outward; spiritual, and not sensible. Though really present in the disciples, this other Paraclete would not be seen by the world, as Christ Himself had been seen, and yet in Him, Christ unseen would be present.

All that the Lord Jesus had done for the disciples, the Holy Spirit would continue to do. (In this connection it is interesting to note that He bears the same title as the ascended Lord. The word "Paraclete" is translated "Advocate" in I John 2:1, where we discover that the Lord Jesus Himself is the believer's Advocate at the Father's right hand.) If the Redeemer had taught them, guided them, strengthened them, the Holy Spirit would continue to do this, and even more. The blessed, august Person is to be to the disciples and to the Church all that Christ would have been had He tarried among them, and had been the personal companion, counsellor and help of each one of them. Yes, His work in us is to make Christ as real to us as though He walked by our side; to so continue His presence to us that the gap may be filled between the open grave and the exalted throne; between the risen Master and the Man in the Glory. Yes, to so continue that presence that Christ Himself shall minister to our needs as though we looked Him in the face, felt the sympathy of His shining tears, and caught the touch of His guiding Hand.

The vital truth in the Upper Room discourse is, that *just as the Lord Jesus is able to meet every need of the*

19

sinner, so the Holy Spirit is able to meet every need of the believer. Oh that this blessed truth could be grasped and apprehended by every child of God! This is where the Church is sorely divided today. Comparatively few evangelicals believe this glorious fact. Yet, this was the good news of the coming of the Spirit, as the Spirit of the risen exalted Lord. The believer has now the Spirit of Sonship. "And because ye are sons, God hath sent forth the Spirit of his Son into your hearts, crying, Abba, Father" (Gal. 4:6). How amazing that the very same blessed Spirit that inhabited the temple of the Son of God now indwells us. That is how we can become like Christ; that is how we can live a victorious Christian life.

The disciples were sorrowful. The announcement of the Saviour's intended departure had left them in a dejected, forlorn condition. His joyful message to them was, "I will not leave you comfortless" (John 14:8). "I will not leave you friendless" (Knox). "I will not leave you desolate" (A.R.V.). "I will not leave you bereaved" (Weymouth). "I will not leave you forlorn" (Moffat). Oh, how many desolate, forlorn Christians there are who are living as if they are friendless and as spiritual orphans! "Let not your heart be disquieted," says their Lord, "Because I have said these things unto you, sorrow hath filled your heart. But I have wonderful news for you: I will request of the Father another Comforter, and He will meet all your need." The message of John fourteen is not for a funeral sermon alone; it is a message for all disturbed, confused, lonely, downcast believers. In these chapters we find that the Holy Spirit would meet three vital needs of disciples at that time:

1. In isolation—"I will pray the Father and He shall give you another Comforter, that He may abide with you forever" (John 14:16).

2. In ignorance—"He shall teach you all things" (John 14:26).
"He will guide you into all truth" (John 16:13).

3. In impotence—"When He is come, He will convict the world. . ." (John 16:8).

Oh how the lonely sentinel of the Cross of Christ in a heathen land needs the support of the Comforter! Cut off from Christian fellowship, separated from home and loved ones, oftentimes having a definite fight of faith regarding finance, and "dwelling where Satan's seat is" (Rev. 2:13); exposed to all the assaults of the demons of hell, he desperately needs the ministry of the Paraclete. How often, as a pioneer missionary in Eastern Europe, have I longed for Christian fellowship when the nearest foreign missionary was several hundred miles away. As I laboured alone for years in tremendously needy mission fields, I proved again and again the support of the Paraclete. Recently, in North Africa we visited a lonely sister at her mission station—the only one for Christ in that Moslem city. We found her in distress over a problem which would only confront a missionary in an Islam mission field. She had no human companionship, but in her extremity she found the sufficiency of the Holy Spirit to meet her peculiar need.

Thank God, He can also meet the need of our ignorance. It is not possible for every one of us to go to a Bible School or Seminary, but even so, we may have an anointing from the Spirit that we may know the things of God (I John 2:20,27). As a boy preacher, beginning to evangelize at fourteen years of age, I had not the privilege of attending Bible School, but was cast upon the Holy Spirit for the knowledge of divine truth. The mighty Spurgeon, although he founded a Pastors' College, was not the product of a Bible Institution. However, even with human instructors at Bible Colleges,

21

one is thrown back upon the Spirit for spiritual illumination. No matter what one's opportunity in education may be, it is the birthright privilege of every believer to be instructed in the things of God through the divine Spirit. The best way to know our Bible is to read it on our knees under the Spirit's anointing. Our prayer daily should be, "Oh, Thou blessed Spirit of Truth, teach me."

As the Spirit of Truth—

(1) He speaks nothing but the truth; (2) He inspires the truth; (3) He reveals the truth.

It is possible for a student to have a thorough understanding of the Hebrew and Greek languages, and Scripture truth carefully classified in his mind from Genesis to Revelation, and yet not be taught of the Spirit. During an evangelistic campaign on the borders of England and Scotland several years ago, I had a blind boy of seventeen years conducting the daily Bible readings. He studied his Bible in Braille. He had had very little practical education, yet it was a sheer joy for preachers to listen to him expound the Scriptures. In my boyhood days in Scotland I knew a sanitary inspector who had a greater grasp of the deep things of God than many of the theological professors in the universities.

Spiritual truth is only spiritually discerned. "Mere man, with his natural gifts cannot take in the thoughts of God's Spirit; they seem mere folly to him, and he cannot grasp them, because they demand a scrutiny which is spiritual" (I Cor. 2:14 Knox).

Again, *the blessed Spirit meets the need of our impotence*. The meaning of our Saviour's words is that when the Spirit of Pentecost comes to dwell in the heart and life of the disciples, through their vital witness the Spirit will convict the worldlings of their damning sin of unbelief in Christ. How many believers make alibis and excuses for their powerlessness in Christian testimony as being backward, shy or nervous. We must remember that the Christian life is not a natural life, but a supernatural one. Only the Holy Ghost can win souls to the Lord Jesus Christ. The disciples were commanded not to evangelize until the Holy Ghost had come (Acts 1:8). The reason is obvious. There could be no conviction of sin, no repentance, no regeneration apart from Him. In John 15:26-27 we are clearly told that it is our unspeakable privilege to witness to a crucified, rejected Lord, but this must be done in partnership with the Spirit of Truth. *The Holy Spirit is the great Evangelist of the Son of God.* Actually, He ought not to be here: the Saviour ought to be here. The Spirit is here because Christ was rejected. The Holy Spirit came on the day of Pentecost to empower the disciples with holy unction for the task of evangelism and personal witness. We may have the eloquence of a Demosthenes, but unless we are empowered by the Spirit of God, our words are in vain. We must testify to the unsaved "with the Holy Ghost sent down from heaven " (I Peter 1:12).

Oh dear timid believer, who longs to witness for your blessed Lord, step out in the path of obedience, depending entirely on the Spirit to speak through you. Even if you give your witness with halting, stammering words, the Holy Ghost will bless it to the salvation of souls. Some years ago a very retiring old man approached a young sportsman about his soul. The young man, as an Olympic sprinter, was filled with his own glory until the quiet, halting words of the servant of God were used of the Holy Ghost to convict him of sin. The young man became an evangelist in Scotland, and won hundreds of souls to the Lord. His ministry is carried on today through the lives of these precious souls.

The reason why so many believers' lives are a grief

and disappointment to them is that they are seeking to live the Christian life apart from the Spirit. During the time of revival in Hungary, a young Salvation Army girl in Budapest came into the meetings held for defeated Christians. I asked her what was her problem. With great distress she told me that she truly loved the Lord, but she had no desire to pray, and to read the Bible was a drudgery. I said to her, "Some years ago I visited a famous European art gallery one Saturday afternoon, without a guide. I was keenly disappointed and bored. I said to myself as I came down the steps of the building, 'I do not know why people come from all parts of the world to visit this place.' Some time later I was invited by believers in that city to tour the same gallery as their guest. They employed a guide, and under his skillful instruction the tapestries and paintings came alive. I was thrilled beyond words, and kept saying to myself, "Wonderful! wonderful! No wonder people come from all parts of the world to visit this place!" Then I remembered my previous experience. I said to the young sister, "What made the difference?" She smiled as she exclaimed with a beaming face, "I see it now. It was the guide!" Oh how many Christians there are who are trying to pray, study the Word, and witness, apart from the Holy Ghost!

"But why should the Saviour go away?" was surely the thought in the hearts of His disciples, "Why could He not stay with us and do these things for us?" Seeing them still perplexed, their Lord says to them, "It is expedient for you that I go away." How startling and strange must these words have seemed as they fell upon the ears of the already baffled disciples. How could it be expedient or profitable for them? What could be more glorious than the actual earthly presence of their Master?

"My Saviour, can it ever be
That I should gain by losing Thee?"

A Jewish doctor, saved in our meetings some years ago on the Continent, as a young believer was sorely tried by Satan. One day in his distress he came to me and exclaimed, "Oh, I wish Christ were alive today and lived here in our city, and in my home. If I had His constant companionship, what a wonderful Christian I could be." I understood immediately the longings of his heart. Coming to the Scripture, I showed him that Christ taught that the mystical, supernatural, indwelling Presence of God, the Holy Ghost, is a far greater blessing than His own earthly Presence.

"It is to your advantage that I go away" (Weymouth), said the Saviour. The Lord Jesus Christ, in human flesh, could only be in one place at a time. We remember how the beloved sister cried in sorrow, "Lord, if thou hadst been here, my brother had not died." But now, by the Spirit, the Lord Jesus Christ is present everywhere. "For where two or three are gathered together in My Name, there am I in the midst of them." Christ, in outward companionship, could not be so much to them, nor do so much for them, as He would through intimate communion with them by the Spirit, after His saving work was accomplished.

It was not only to their advantage that the Saviour should go back to the Father, via Calvary, but it was also necessary. In this connection the words of John 7:39 are illuminating, "The Holy Ghost was not yet given; because that Jesus was not yet glorified." A. J. Gordon sweetly reasons: "If the Spirit is simply the measure of the Son, His sole work being to communicate the work of the Son, what gain could there be in the departure of the one in order for the coming of the other? Would it not be simply the exchange of Christ for Christ—His visible presence for His invisible? To us the answer to this question is most obvious. It was not the earthly Christ whom the Holy Ghost was to communicate to the Church, but the *heavenly* Christ;—the Christ re-invested with His eternal power, re-clothed with the glory which He had with the Father before the world was, and re-endowed with the infinite treasures of grace which He had purchased by His death on the Cross. It is as though—to use a very inadequate illustration—a beloved father were to say to his family: 'My children, I have provided well for your needs; but your condition is one of poverty compared with what it may become. By the death of a kinsman in my native country, I have become heir to an immense estate. If you will submit cheerfully to my leaving you and crossing the sea, and entering into my inheritance, I will send you back a thousand times more than you could have by my remaining with you.' Only, in the instance we are considering, Christ is the testator as well as the heir. By His death, the inheritance became available, and when He had ascended into heaven, He sent down the Holy Spirit to distribute the estate among those who were joint-heirs with Him. The divine wealth only became completely available on the death, resurrection and ascension of our Lord; so that the Holy Spirit, the divine Conveyancer, had not the full inheritance to convey until Jesus was glorified. Christ at God's right hand will have more to give than while on earth; therefore the Church will have more to receive through the Paraclete than through the visible Christ."

Until Christ's earthly work had been accomplished, the Spirit's work could not begin. The office of the Spirit is to communicate Christ to us in His entirety. Without the expiatory work of Christ for us, the sanctifying work of the Spirit in us would be impossible. The redemptive work of Christ is the basis of all the operations of the Spirit. There could be no Pentecost had there been no Calvary.

Not only must Christ be glorified at the Father's right hand, but the Spirit was to glorify Him on the earth. This would be done by the Spirit of Truth taking the things of Christ and revealing them unto His disciples. "It will be for Him, the truth-giving Spirit, when He comes, to guide you into all truth. He will not utter a message of His own; He will utter the message that has been given to Him; and He will make plain to you what is still to come. And He will bring honour to Me, because it is from Me that He will derive what He makes plain to you. I say that He will derive from Me what He makes plain to you, because all that belongs to the Father belongs to Me." (Knox).

The Spirit is the custodian of all things belonging to Christ; to Him is committed the cause and credit of the Son of God. He is well entitled to take of what is Christ's especially considering that it is what the Father has that is Christ's, because He Himself is a divine Person, co-equal in power and glory with the Son. He is also qualified and able to receive what is Christ's because, as a member of the Trinity, He was in the great Council Chamber in the by-gone eternity when the glorious plan of redemption was conceived. Also He is a blessed Person whom Christ loves and can trust in this great undertaking. The Saviour sets His stamp of approval alone upon the blessed Spirit. As the Father could say, "This is my beloved Son, in whom I am well pleased," so the Redeemer was satisfied and pleased with the work of the Spirit in His own ministry. Yes, and only the Spirit knows the "all things" of Christ!

The resources at the disposal of the Holy Spirit are

boundless and eternal. The perfect knowledge possessed by the Spirit of our Lord's mediatorial work
placed Him in a position infinitely superior to all others
as a witness and testifier to Jesus Christ. We dare to
affirm that the Holy Spirit only could entirely glorify the
Son of God. In reading carefully and prayerfully the
precious prophecies of the Redeemer in the Upper
Room, we see standing out before us the fact that the
whole sum of the Spirit's ministry would culminate in
the glory of the beloved Son. "He shall glorify Me." The
Spirit glorifies Christ by taking of the things of Christ
and revealing them unto us. All the gifts and graces of
the Spirit, all the preaching and the writings of the
apostles under the influence of the Spirit, the tongues
and the miracles, were to glorify Christ. As J. C. Hare
has clearly stated, *The Comforter, in every part of His
three-fold work, glorifies Christ. In convincing us of
sin, He convinces us of the sin of not believing in Christ.
In convincing us of righteousness, He convinces us of
the righteousness of Christ: of that righteousness which
was made manifest in Christ going to the Father, and
which He received to bestow on all who would believe
in Him. And lastly, in convincing of judgment, He convinces us that the prince of the world was judged in
the life and by the death of Christ."

The old Puritan, John Goodwin, has said: "What
things of His doth our Saviour mean the Holy Ghost
shall take and show? Doubtless they are such things of
His, or relating unto Him, which are contained and
asserted in the Gospels, as His divine nature, human
nature—His incarnation, conception, birth, holiness of
life, miracles, death, resurrection, ascension—with all
the ends and great purposes and intentions of God in
this whole dispensation of Him, etc. Now, our Saviour's
meaning is that the Holy Ghost shall take all these and

show them unto them—therefore, should declare, open, and interpret them unto them, and cause them to understand and consider the way, worth, and beneficial tendencies of them unto men and women. And indeed, this is the proper work of the Holy Ghost, to show unto men and women the things that are of Jesus Christ, and to cause them to understand them, to draw out the hearts and judgments of men, and raise in them holy purposes and resolutions—and so likewise to draw out from them holy practices and actions; for this is the gracious and heavenly work of the Holy Ghost, too; so that where He is not furnished with these things of Jesus Christ, where He hath no opportunity of showing these things unto men, He hath little to do; He taketh no pleasure to abide there, as artificiers or workmen care not to dwell or work in such places where proper materials are either scarce or not to be had."

In the New Testament the Holy Spirit takes of the treasures of Christ and reveals them unto us:

In the Gospels, He shows us the moral glories of the Man, Christ Jesus.

In Romans, He reveals to us the perfect work and righteousness of the Saviour.

In Ephesians, He reveals our heavenly position in our ascended Lord.

In Colossians, He unfolds treasures of wisdom and knowledge in Him.

In Hebrews, He unveils before our wondering gaze the glory of His Priesthood, after the order of Melchisedec.

In Peter's Epistles, He tells of the preciousness of Christ to the devoted believer.

In the Revelation, He makes real before our eyes the triumphant glory of the Lamb, as it had been slain.

29

The Spirit glorifies the Son, not in His Person, as that had already been done by the Father. Peter said, "God gave Him glory" (I Peter 1:21) when He raised Him from the dead. *The Spirit would glorify the Son in the lives of the believers and in the local assemblies.* As it pleased the Father that in Him should all fulness dwell (Col. 1:19), so it is the province of the Spirit to unfold that fulness to the adoring eyes of the saints. It is a glorious experience to be conducted by the Holy Spirit into the blessed views of the offices of the Lord Jesus as Prophet, Priest and King. When the Spirit communicates to us the glories of Christ, we are drawn into a vital relationship with our Lord. In adoration we prostrate ourselves before Him and crown Him Lord of all. The beauties of Christ are revealed in us to the unsaved.

> "God in heaven hath a treasure,
>   Riches none may count or tell,
> Hath a deep eternal pleasure,
>   Christ the Son He loveth well.
>
> God hath here on earth a treasure.
>   None but He its price may know,
> Deep unfathomable pleasure,
>   Christ revealed in saints below!"

Ralph Erskine, referring to this truth, says that "In the Father, the honey is in the flower which is at such a distance from us that we could never extract it. In the Son, the honey is in the comb, prepared for us by our Emmanuel, God-man, Redeemer, the Word that was made flesh, saying 'All things that the Father hath are mine, and for your use and behoof;' it is in the comb. But then, next we have the honey in the mouth; the Spirit taking all things and making application thereof, by showing them unto us, and making us eat and drink

30

with Christ, and share of these "all things;" yea, not only eat the honey, but the honey-comb with the honey; not only His benefits, but Himself!"

Thus, we are reminded that *the Spirit also glorifies Christ by making our Lord precious and real to us.* In the measure that we allow the Holy Spirit, through meditation, prayer, and obedience, to take of the things of Christ and make them precious to us, do we glorify Him by our dynamic Christian witness. It is an utter impossibility to be an effective witness for Christ unless the Lord Jesus Christ is in us a "living bright reality."

> Lord, Thou hast made Thyself to me
> A living bright reality,
> More present to faith's vision keen
> Than any earthly object seen;
> More dear, more intimately nigh
> Than e'en the closest earthly tie.

As we have already stated, the Christian life is a supernatural, mystical life. We have never seen Christ with the naked eye, yet we would gladly die for Him. He is the altogether lovely One. This is the miraculous work of the Holy Spirit in our souls. It was He Who in the first place gave us a sight of the dying Lamb of Calvary. It was He Who drew out our heart's affections to that blessed One, so that we can exclaim like Paul in soul rapture, "The Son of God, who loved me and gave Himself for me" (Gal. 2:20).

The twin marks of a Spirit-filled believer are a deep appreciation for the Person of our Lord Jesus, and a deep, spiritual, reverential hunger for an insight into the Word of God. Anything less is only a sham. How solemn, then, is our responsibility in the light of this glorious truth, and in the light of a dying world, to allow the Spirit daily to effect this blessed work in our souls. "He

31

shall glorify Me."

The question arises, when did our Lord Jesus pray for the Paraclete? He said, "I will pray the Father. . ." This word "pray" is not, as it were, a beggar making a petition to a king, but rather a request from a person of the same equality. We eagerly scan the whole discourse of our Lord to His disciples, as found in these chapters, and discover to our dismay that no prayer is recorded. Surely, in the seventeenth chapter, in His great High-priestly prayer, He will request this of the Father. But no! He asks for every conceivable blessing for the disciples, but the greatest gift of all He did not pray for. Why? I say it reverently, He could not. "For the Holy Spirit was not yet given, because that Jesus was not yet glorified" (John 7:39). The Saviour says repeatedly in the Upper Room, "I go unto My Father" (John 20: 17). He looked over the Cross to the life beyond it. His gaze was onward to the Mediatorial Throne, and to His all-prevailing intercession within the Veil. The sacrifice was not only to be offered on earth, but pleaded in the courts above. In other words, the Lord Jesus Christ must present the blood of His atoning sacrifice to His Father (Hebrews 9:12, 24) before the Spirit could be bestowed to the Church. This is Peter's explanation of the phenomena of Pentecost, "And now, exalted at God's right hand, He has claimed from His Father His promise to bestow the Spirit" (Acts 2:33 Knox).

It seems that in the eternal counsels of the Godhead, the suffering, obedient Son and Saviour was promised the ascension gift of the glorious Spirit in the fulfilment of His death on the Cross. God, for the sake of our Saviour's honour, and for the glory of His undertaking had, in His wisdom, determined that so incomparably excellent a gift should be the reward of His obedience, the consequence of His triumph, the effect of His intercession above, an ornament of His royal state, a pledge of His princely munificence; it was reserved as a most rich and majestic gratuity, fit to be conferred at His coronation when He solemnly was inaugurated to sovereign dignity and invested with power superlative.

The Holy Spirit was the Father's coronation love-gift to His beloved Son. We may imagine the Father saying to Him, "I thank Thee, my beloved Son, for being obedient unto death; executing My plans and purposes. And now I give Thee the Holy Spirit for those whom Thou hast redeemed by Thy blood."

The Spirit is the all-inclusive gift from the Father to the Son, and the crowning gift of the Son to the Church. "But the Comforter, which is the Holy Ghost, Whom the Father will send in My name" (John 14:26) "The Comforter. . . Whom I will send unto you from the Father" (John 15:25). That is why the Spirit is so precious to me. That is why I worship Him and commune with Him and appreciate Him in His condescension (II Cor. 13:14).

Who prayed down the Spirit of Pentecost? Was it the one hundred and twenty disciples in the Upper Room? By no means! Though it is true, as we see in the first chapter of the Acts, there were fervent, earnest prayer meetings, when the disciples prepared their hearts for the coming of the Spirit, nevertheless, *it was the glorified Son Who prayed down the Spirit.* I would not, for one single moment, minimize the necessity for our personal heart-preparation for the fulness of the Holy Ghost in our lives, but I am zealous for the honour and glory of my blessed Lord, when I state unequivocally that it was in answer to *His* prayer the Spirit came. He came on the basis of the finished redemptive work of the Son and His glorification at the Father's right hand.

I often think that the Church meditates too little on

the ascension of Christ. In searching through various hymn books, one is startled to find so few hymns devoted exclusively to this blessed theme. There are a few fine Russian, German, Scandinavian and French hymns, along with those in the English language, which magnify Christ in His ascension. We treasure every one of them. One of the finest in the English language is by T. Kelly:

> Look, ye saints, the sight is glorious:
> See the Man of Sorrows now;
> From the fight return'd victorious,
> Every knee to Him shall bow:
> Crown Him, crown Him!
> Crowns become the Victor's brow.

> Crown the Saviour! angels, crown Him!
> Rich the trophies Jesus brings;
> In the seat of power enthrone Him,
> While the vault of heaven rings:
> Crown Him, crown Him!
> Crown the Saviour King of kings.

> Sinners in derision crowned Him,
> Mocking thus the Saviour's claim;
> Saints and angels crowd around Him,
> Own His title, praise His name:
> Crown Him, crown Him!
> Spread abroad the Victor's fame.

> Hark! those bursts of acclamation;
> Hark! those loud triumphant chords;
> Jesus takes the highest station:
> Oh, what joy the sight affords!
> Crown Him, crown Him!
> King of kings, and Lord of lords.

It was direct from this scene of His triumphant entry, when He was "received up into glory" (I Timothy 3: 16), that the Holy Spirit was sent forth in His Name.

It is not for us now to pray God to send down the Holy Spirit from heaven, but for us to joyfully appropriate the blessed truth that the Comforter *has* come, as the Spirit of the risen, glorified Christ. *Pentecost is just as much a reality as Calvary.* The Mediator of the New Covenant can never die on the Cross of Calvary again, and the Holy Spirit can never become incarnate again in the Church of Jesus Christ. Just as in Bethlehem was the incarnation of the Son, so at Pentecost was the incarnation of the Spirit. However, though it is true that Calvary and Pentecost are two historical acts of God which will never be repeated, let us remember that the blessing of Calvary and the blessing of Pentecost continue for and in the Church until her Home-call (I Thess. 4:16).

As an unsaved person repents of his sin and receives Christ as his Lord and Saviour, and has an individual Calvary experience, so every time a believer, realizing his own pitifully inadequate spiritual experience, seeks a renewing of the Holy Ghost, he comes to know the blessing of Pentecost again in his own life. We who preach the Gospel, believe that the precious blood of our Redeemer is just as efficacious now as it was nearly two thousand years ago. In the same way, we believe that the Spirit's definite work is as efficacious now in the believer, as it was in the lives of the disciples on the day of Pentecost. We make bold to say that, just as we had an individual Calvary experience when we first met the Saviour, so it is our glorious privilege and responsibility to have a Pentecostal experience upon the reception of the fulness of the Spirit.

Pentecost commemorates to each succeeding generation the gift of the Holy Spirit. The grace conferred on that blessed company, waiting breathlessly and prayerfully for His advent, is the measure of the Church's privilege to the end of the age.

My plea, as I have dwelt on the wonders of Calvary and Pentecost, is that the Church will once again appropriate all the blessings bought by our Lord and brought down by the Spirit at Pentecost. In this manner, every one of us desperately needs an individual Pentecost.

James A. McConkey, of blessed memory, whose writings greatly influenced my mother in times of deep trial, tells a striking story:

"I was standing on the wall of a great lock. Outside was a huge lake vessel about to enter. At my feet lay the empty lock—waiting. For what? Waiting to be filled. Away beyond lay great Lake Superior with its limitless abundance of supply, also waiting. Waiting for what? Waiting for something to be done at the lock ere the great lake could pour in its fulness. In a moment it was done. The lock-keeper reached out his hand and touched a steel lever. A little wicket gate sprang open under the magic touch. At once the water in the lock began to boil and seethe. As it seethed I saw it rapidly creeping up the walls of the lock. In a few moments the lock was full. The great gates swung open and the huge ship floated into the lock now filled to the brim with the fulness inpoured from the waiting lake without.

"Is not this a picture of a great truth about the Holy Spirit? Here are God's children, like that empty lock, waiting to be filled. And, as that inland sea outside the lock was willing and waiting to pour its abundance into the lock, so here is God willing to pour His fulness of life into the lives of His children. But He is waiting. For what? Waiting, as the lake waited, for something to be done by us. Waiting for us to reach forth and touch that tiny wicket gate of consecration through which His

36

abundant life shall flow and fill. Is it hard to move? Does the rust of worldliness corrode it? Is the will stubborn, and slow to yield? Yet God is waiting for it. And once it is done, He reveals Himself in fulness of life, even as He has promised; even as He has been all the time willing and ready to do. For all the barriers and hindrances have been upon our side; not upon His. They are the barriers, not of His unwillingness, but of our unyieldedness."

In conclusion, let us make it clear that there is a vast difference in our possessing the Spirit of God and the Spirit of God possessing us. It is the difference between the man who goes into a house as a guest, and the one who goes in as the owner and host, having absolute authority and possession. Years ago there was a ministerial conference in the city of Philadelphia to decide upon the evangelist for a united campaign. Different names were mentioned, and then one minister brought forth that of D. L. Moody. Another preacher rather sarcastically said, "Do you think that Mr. Moody has a monopoly on the Holy Ghost?" "No," was the sincere reply, "but I believe that the Holy Ghost has a monopoly of D. L. Moody." There is a difference.

The burning question is, has the Holy Spirit a monopoly of me today?

Three

He is Come

"When the Lord Christ had finished his work, was received up into glory, and seated on the right hand of God, and all the elect angels and redeemed of the Lord within the vail had been spectators of His coronation and exaltation, and sung, 'Worthy is the Lamb that was slain', he asked of and received from the Father the promise of the Holy Ghost. And our Lord's first act after his entrance into the holiest of all, and when seated on his Mediatorial throne, was to bestow the Holy Ghost, and shed him abundantly in his gifts and graces on his apostles and saints on the day of Pentecost as the great promise of the New Testament. The doctrine of this was first published after the inauguration of

Christ in heaven by the immediate grace and revelation of the Holy Ghost, who accompanied it with his effectual power, promise, and blessing, turning sinners by it 'from darkness unto light and from the power of Satan unto God.'"

Samuel Eyles Pierce

Oh spread the tidings 'round
 Wherever man is found,
Wherever human hearts
 And human woes abound;
Let every Christian tongue
 Proclaim the joyful sound:
THE COMFORTER HAS COME!

Pentecost was the fulfilment of the promise of the Redeemer in the Upper Room. The Saviour had repeatedly said, "When He is come . . . ," thus preparing the disciples for the advent of the Spirit. Some of them could have reasoned, "Is the Spirit not already here? Has He not been carrying on a blessed ministry from the beginning of creation? What does our Lord mean when He says, 'When He is come'?" The answer is that until now He had come as a transient Guest; now, He would come to abide. It is as if a tourist visiting a country were to say to his friends there that when he would come he would carry out certain transactions. His friends would immediately reply in astonishment, "What do you mean by saying when you come? You are here now!" "I mean," he replies, "that I am coming here to abide as a permanent citizen in this country. When I come I will accomplish this work." In the same manner, the eternal Spirit would come as a permanent Guest to abide in the Church.

The glorious truth of Pentecost is that on that day God, the Holy Ghost, came down from heaven in answer to the request of the ascended Lord. "Therefore, being

41

by the right hand of God exalted, and having received of the Father the promise of the Holy Ghost, He hath shed forth this which ye now see and hear" (Acts 2:33). As Augustine has said, "Therefore the Holy Ghost this day—Pentecost—descended into the temple of His apostles which He had prepared for Himself, appearing no more as a transient visitor, but as a perpetual Comforter and as an eternal inhabitant. He came, therefore, on this day to His disciples, no longer by the grace of visitation and operation, but by the VERY PRESENCE OF HIS MAJESTY."

Just as distinctively and as definitely as the Son of God came as a Person unto Bethlehem, so the Spirit of God came as a definite Person at Pentecost. As in Bethlehem the incarnation of the Son took place, so Pentecost was, in one sense, the incarnation of the eternal Spirit. The Lord Jesus had a body prepared for Him (Hebrews 10:5). "Ah," but you say, "the Holy Spirit has no body." Oh yes He has; the Church is "the habitation of God through the Spirit" (Ephes. 2:22). Each individual member's body is His temple: "What, know ye not that your body is the temple of the Holy Ghost which is in you, which ye have of God, and ye are not your own . . . ?" (I Cor. 6:19). As the Son of God became incarnate by union with a real human body, born of the Virgin, so there is a sense in which the Holy Ghost becomes incarnate by uniting Himself with the human bodies of men and women who believe in Christ. Here is the continuation of the Incarnation: God dwelling in human flesh!

We hasten to state that the Spirit's union with the believer is not a natural, personal one, so that the apostles and the Spirit became one person, as the Manhood and Godhead are one in Christ. The saints are not called by the name of the Spirit, but are said to be "spiritual," and the Holy Ghost is not said to be "made man," but to "dwell" in man. The Lord Jesus manifested Himself through His own personality; the Holy Ghost expresses Himself through ours. What a sublime mystery is the truth of the incarnation of the Spirit! Oh, what sovereign grace! To think that the Father could so love us as to send Christ to die for us, and then send His Spirit into our hearts to abide. In Galatians 4:4-6 we see the two-fold gift of the Father, thus uniting Pentecost with Bethlehem: "God sent forth His Son . . . God hath sent forth the Spirit of His Son." Meditate well, oh my brother and my sister, on this sublime truth, that your body is the Cathedral of the Holy Ghost. Oftentimes, when ministering the Word in the large cathedrals of northern Europe, I have delighted in telling the assembled saints that their own bodies were the cathedrals of the Spirit of God, and not these vast buildings of great architectural beauty.

We now live in the Pentecostal Age, in the dispensation of the Spirit, when He is personally dwelling in the Church on earth as really as Christ dwelt among men in the days of His flesh. It is sad that a vast number of evangelicals are living on the other side of Pentecost, as if that great event had never occurred. They are living on the same plane as lived the early disciples before that day. Historically and chronologically they are on this side, but experimentally they are on the other side. This mental attitude is portrayed in many of our hymns. From childhood I have been astonished to discover that the majority of our hymns in relation to the Spirit are pre-Pentecostal in their outlook. As we read line by line, and verse by verse, we can come to no other conclusion than that the authors had no clear grasp of the present dispensation of the Spirit; that the Holy Spirit, as the Spirit of Sonship is now in the

Church communicating the risen life of Christ to the members of His body, and empowering them to take the Gospel to every creature. Many of these hymns begin with the word, "Come", beseeching the Spirit to come down from heaven. If this is scriptural, why not sing hymns beseeching Christ to come down from heaven and die on the cross of Calvary again? "Oh," you say, "but that would be false doctrine!" Indeed it would, because "This man, after He had offered one sacrifice for sins forever, sat down at the right hand of God on high " (Hebrews 10:12). His is a finished work! Is it not a strange thing, then, to beseech the Holy Spirit to come to the Church, when He has already come?

C. H. Spurgeon, in one of the few hymns he wrote, enters into the truth of the present indwelling of the Spirit:

> The Holy Ghost is here,
>   Where saints in prayer agree:
> As Jesu's parting gift He's near
>   Each pleading company.
>
> Not far away is He,
>   To be by prayer brought nigh,
> But here in present majesty
>   As in His courts on high.
>
> He dwells within our soul,
>   An ever-welcome Guest:
> He reigns with absolute control
>   As monarch in the breast.
>
> Our bodies are His shrine,
>   And He the indwelling Lord:
> All hail, Thou Comforter Divine,
>   Be evermore adored!
>
> Obedient to Thy will,
>   We want to feel Thy power,
> O Lord of Life, our hopes fulfill,
>   And bless this hallowed hour.

Then there is another class of hymns which begin with "Come", or some such similar expression, which on first sight seem unscriptural. When one enters into the spirit of the hymn, however, he can feel the longing of the author for a richer, deeper, fuller experience of the Holy Ghost in his life. Or, under a burden for the condition of a "dying Sardis" church, he feels that there is need of a definite realization of the Spirit's presence and power in the midst. The invocation is not for the Spirit to come down from heaven, but that the incarnate Spirit, already inhabiting the Church of God, will "break forth" in a mighty manifestation of Himself. "And when they had prayed, the place was shaken where they were assembled together, and they were all filled with the Holy Ghost, and they spake the word of God with boldness, ... and with great power gave the apostles witness of the resurrection of the Lord Jesus: and great grace was upon them all" (Acts 4:31-33).

The early Moravians and Methodists wrote such hymns, and who can deny that God answered their prayers in sending them mighty manifestations of His grace! They witnessed revival because they earnestly sought the Spirit. The chief Moravian hymn writer, James Montgomery, well illustrates our point:

> Lord God, the Holy Ghost,
>   In this accepted hour,
> As on the day of Pentecost
>   Descend in all Thy power.
>
> We meet with one accord
>   In our appointed place,
> And wait the promise of our Lord,
>   The Spirit of all grace.
>
> Like mighty rushing wind
>   Upon the waves beneath,
> Move with one impulse every mind,
>   One soul, one feeling breathe.

45

The young, the old inspire
　　With wisdom from above:
And give us hearts and tongues of fire
　　To pray and praise and love.

Spirit of light explore,
　　And chase our gloom away;
With lustre shining more and more,
　　Unto the perfect day.

Spirit of truth, be Thou
　　In life and death our Guide;
O Spirit of adoption, now
　　May we be sanctified.

Joseph Hart, to my mind, was as great an expositor of the Scriptures among the Calvinists, as was C. H. Spurgeon. No one could deny that he had a great spiritual insight into the truth. Yet, among his many hymns, we find the following:

Come, Holy Spirit, come,
　　Let Thy bright beams arise;
Dispel the darkness from our minds,
　　And open all our eyes.

Convince us of our sin,
　　Then lead to Jesus' blood,
And to our wondering view reveal
　　The secret love of God.

Show us that loving Man
　　That rules the courts of bliss,
The Lord of hosts, the mighty God,
　　The eternal Prince of Peace.

'Tis Thine to cleanse the heart,
　　To sanctify the soul,
To pour fresh life in every part
　　And new create the whole.

Dwell, therefore, in our hearts,
　　Our minds from bondage free;
Then we shall know, and praise, and love,
　　The Father, Son, and Thee.

46

During the days of revival in Latvia, Poland, Czecho-slovakia, Hungary and Bulgaria, the believers sang again and again, with tears streaming down their cheeks:

> Into my heart, into my heart,
>> Come into my heart, Lord Jesus;
> Come in today, come in to stay,
>> Come into my heart, Lord Jesus.

They knew that He had already come into their hearts. They were conscious of the glory of this experi-ence as new-born babes, but their longing was for a deeper and fuller appreciation and apprehension of the Person of Christ in their lives. Thus they continued to sing this little chorus. Were they not in apostolic suc-cession? Even Paul prayed for the saints at Ephesus: "That Christ may dwell in your hearts by faith." Surely when these believers were born again Christ came to dwell in them in the Person of the Holy Spirit. We understand the prayer better when we realize that the word "dwell" comes from two Greek words meaning "down" and "home". In other words, Paul was praying that the Lord Jesus would be able to settle down and make His home in the hearts of the believers, filling, and ruling consciously every part of the life. Might it not be, in like manner, that writers such as Joseph Hart, who prayed, "Dwell, therefore, within our hearts", had in mind the same longing?

I believe that a profound change would come over the entire blood-washed Church of Jesus Christ, if each believer would realize that we are now living in the blessed days of the Holy Ghost's personal administra-tion. If every pastor, Bible teacher, evangelist, and Sun-day School teacher would begin now to teach all that was involved in the Spirit's advent, I am quite sure that this recognition of His Person would revolutionize our lives, and that once again Pentecostal days of blessing would come.

Mr. Spurgeon cried fervently to his flock, as he pleaded for a recognition of the Spirit's presence: "Death and condemnation to a church that is not yearning after the Spirit, and crying and groaning until the Spirit has wrought mightily in her midst. He is here; He has never gone back since He descended at Pentecost. He is often grieved and vexed, for He is peculiarly jealous and sensitive, and the one sin never forgiven has to do with His blessed Person; therefore let us be very tender towards Him, walk humbly before Him, wait on Him very earnestly, and resolve that there should be nothing knowingly continued which would prevent Him working in our midst.

"Brethren, if we do not have the Spirit of God, it were better to shut the churches, to nail up the doors, to put a black cross on them and say: 'God have mercy on us!' If you ministers have not the Spirit of God, you had better not preach, and you people had better stay at home. I think I speak not too strongly when I say that a church in the land without the Spirit of God is rather a curse than a blessing. This is a solemn word; the Holy Spirit—or nothing, and worse than nothing."

Four

He is Come .... Therefore

"If we believe He is a Person in the Trinity, let us treat Him as a Person, apply ourselves to Him as a Person, glorify Him in our hearts as a Person, dart forth beams of special and peculiar love to, and converse with, Him as a Person. Let us fear to grieve Him and also believe on Him as a Person."
Goodwin

"Less than any other person does He honor Himself. His constant business is to exalt Christ and hide behind His person. Therefore, the Father is pleased when we exalt and honor Him, and He Himself will especially use the instrument which gives Him the glory".
A. B. Simpson

God, the Spirit, we adore Thee,
  In the Trinal Godhead One,
One in love and power and glory
  With the Father and the Son;
Prayer and praise to Thee we bring
  Our devotion's offering.

THE TWO GREAT FUNDAMENTAL FACTS
of Christanity are: firstly, that there is a Man enthroned
at the Father's right hand, and, secondly, that there is a
divine Person indwelling the Church of God on earth.
He is come; therefore, what should be our attitude to
Him?

RECOGNIZE HIM AS A PERSON

Why has a Church more than nineteen hundred years
old not a fuller realization of the witness of the Spirit
than had the Church of the first Century? Surely it is
because the Church today refuses to recognize that the
Holy Spirit came as executive member of the Godhead
on that "natal day" of the Church. In the Acts of the
Apostles we see that the Paraclete is omnipresent in the
great body of Christ, and that the local assemblies and
individual believers recognized Him as a Person. This
book is all aglow with the presence of the Spirit. Peter
said to Ananias, "Why has Satan filled thine heart to
lie to the Holy Ghost? . . . Thou hast not lied unto men
but unto God" (Acts 5:3-5). James, while presiding at
the first general assembly of the evangelical Church,

51

addressed the assembled delegates with these words, "It seemed good to the Holy Ghost and to us." Read where you may, you will see that the apostles' ministry was transformed by the personal advent of the Spirit as predicted by the Redeemer in the Upper Room. As in the four Gospels we see the Lord Jesus at work, so in the Acts of the Apostles we see the Holy Spirit at work. Like the book of Genesis, this book is full of personalities, but the greatest personality of all is "the Lord of the Harvest."

It is interesting to notice that the Holy Spirit refers to Himself as "I" in Jeremiah 31:31-34, (see also Hebrews 10:16), as He employs the personal pronoun to Himself. We find also in the New Testament that:

He can speak	(I Timothy 4:1).
He can invite	(Rev. 22:17).
He can command	(Acts 11:12).
He can forbid	(Acts 16:6).
He can reprove	(John 16:9).
He can teach	(John 14:26).
He can lead	(Romans 8:14).
He can testify	(John 15:26-27).
He can cry	(Galatians 4:6).
He can intercede	(Romans 8:26).
He can approve	(Acts 15:28).
He can witness	(Acts 5:32).
He can give messages	(Rev. 2:7).

As Dr. J. H. Jowett has reminded us, "Let us see to it that we do not so far bow to a tendency as to enthrone a law in the place of a Companion, and exalt a force in place of a Counsellor and Friend. . . . 'A Something not in ourselves that makes for righteousness,' when translated into religious speech, becomes, 'A Friend that sticketh closer than a brother,' and when translated into the New Testament Evangel it becomes the communion of the Holy Ghost. Our fellowship is not with a 'Something', but with a 'Somebody'; not with a force, but with a Spirit; not with 'It', but with 'HIM'. "

Oh, dear brother and sister, have you recognized Him as a Person in your life?

RECEIVE HIM

Some of God's children sincerely believe that because the Spirit has been outpoured upon the Church of God and has never been withdrawn, there is no need for any personal reception of Him. They reason that, having received the Holy Spirit as an indwelling Guest at the time of their regeneration, as the "earnest" and the "seal", there is no necessity for further dealings with Him. "Now if any man have not the Spirit of Christ, he is none of His" (Romans 8:9). "The Spirit Himself beareth witness with our spirit, that we are the children of God" (Romans 8:16 R.V.). "And because ye are sons, God has sent forth the Spirit of His son into your hearts, crying "Abba, Father" (Gal. 4:6). "In whom ye also trusted, after that ye heard the word of truth, the gospel of your salvation; in whom also, after that ye believed, ye were sealed with that Holy Spirit of promise, which is the earnest of our inheritance until the redemption of the purchased possession, unto the praise of His glory" (Ephes. 1:13-14). These friends, however, fail to realize that the Holy Spirit, their Sanctifier, Who comes as the Spirit of Sonship for the believer's walk and work, is a distinct gift from that of the Lord Jesus as Saviour. While it is true that in Galatians 4:4-6 we have the two gifts mentioned together ("God sent forth His Son . . . . God hath sent forth the Spirit of His Son"), yet *there must be a conscious acceptance of each.* As the Lord Jesus is the Father's love-gift to the world, so the Holy Spirit is the Father's love-gift to the

Church. Just as the sin of the world is its rejection of Christ, so the sin of the Church is her ignoring of the Holy Spirit.

WELCOME HIM

We rejoice in the fact that when we received Christ as Lord and Saviour we were supernaturally born again by the Spirit into God's family (John 1:12). By the new birth we were incorporated into Christ (II Cor. 5:17). At the time of our regeneration we became "partakers of the divine nature" by the incoming of the Holy Spirit as the heavenly Guest (II Peter 1:4; I Cor. 6:19-20). Since He became your Guest, have you welcomed Him? Many times a guest has arrived at your home during a very busy season and has lived there for several days before you have been really conscious of his presence. Possibly it was because you were occupied with many things when he first came, that you never sat down and took time to give him a really proper welcome. Then one day you said to him, "Dear friend, you must really forgive us, as we were so occupied with many things on the day of your arrival that we feel we failed to really welcome you. We want now to give you a really hearty welcome to our home. We want to tell you now that the whole house is yours and that we are delighted that you have come to dwell with us." So it is in the lives of many saints. At the time of their regeneration they were occupied possibly exclusively with the joy of sins forgiven and the consequences of the new life, such as breaking with their old companions, and at the same time surveying the vistas of the Christian life. At that time they were not conscious of the Spirit's incoming and indwelling. They failed to welcome Him. Did you welcome Him as a Guest in

54

your heart and life? If not, why not do it just now? Give Him an official welcome on your knees in the secret closet, and say, "Oh, Blessed Paraclete, I bid Thee welcome into the entire temple of my body. I have no secret places; take full control. Carry on Thy blessed work of sanctification."

> Author of our new creation,
>   Giver of the second birth,
> May Thy ceaseless renovation
>   Cleanse our souls from stains of earth:
> And our bodies ever be
>   Holy temples meet for Thee.

ACKNOWLEDGE HIM

In the days when it was well with her, the Church honoured the blessed Spirit. We see such acknowledgment in the early Church. The language of Peter in Acts 11:12 is striking. When explaining his conduct in taking the Gospel to the Gentiles, he simply says, "The Spirit told me to go without hesitation" (R.V.). You remember how Paul witnessed to the weeping elders of Ephesus, "I now go bound in the Spirit unto Jerusalem, not knowing the things that shall befall me there; save that the Holy Ghost witnesseth in every city, saying that bonds and afflictions abide me" (Acts 21:23). Agabus was not ashamed to acknowledge that it was the Holy Spirit who sent warnings to Paul. "A certain prophet, named Agabus . . . and when he was come unto us, he took Paul's girdle, and bound his own hands and feet and said, "Thus saith the Holy Ghost, so shall the Jews at Jerusalem bind the man that owneth this girdle and shall deliver him into the hands of the Gentiles" (Acts 21:10-11).

We believe there is no sin of immodesty committed

55

when a brother or sister reverently testifies in a public gathering that they have had a definite experience with the Holy Spirit. The prophet Micah testified "But truly I am full of power by the Spirit of the Lord" (Micah 3:8).

How many believers say, when they know they have been definitely guided by the Spirit (Romans 8:14), "I felt led" or "I felt an inward urge to do so and so." Such language is not good enough for a child of God. Our testimony must be more definite, or else it is only like the words of an unsaved man. If you sincerely believe that you are led by the Spirit, then why not say so? Why not honour Him?

WORSHIP HIM

When I was a young babe in Christ, I was afraid that if I magnified the Person of the Spirit, possibly the Lord Jesus would be jealous. However, I soon discovered from the reading of the Scriptures that there is no jealousy in the Godhead. Each of the Persons of the Godhead exalts the others, and magnifies the position and work of the others. Each member of the Trinity has a different part to execute in the great plan of Redemption. From the Son we receive everlasting life and we acknowledge it in our praises. For the love we have received from the Father, we return to Him our love and obedience. From the Spirit we receive regeneration and sanctification, and shall we render Him nothing in return—no love, no appreciation, no worship and adoration?

> I worship Thee, Oh Holy Ghost,
> I love to worship Thee
> My risen Lord for aye were lost
> But for Thy company!

OBEY HIM

"The Spirit is the Lord" (II Cor. 3-18 Rotherham).
"For as many as are led by the Spirit of God, they are
the sons of God" (Romans 8:14). It is the constant
privilege of every believer moment by moment to obey
the voice of the Spirit, and thus to walk step by step
with Him (Gal. 5:16). The Paraclete is given, not for
our own spiritual delights, but that we might obey
Him (Acts 5:32). For fresh manifestations of His presence, there must be constant obedience to His dictates.

COMMUNE WITH HIM

No believer can have a dynamic Christian life in
holiness and power, unless he knows the Holy Spirit in
an intimate way. The Lord Jesus, in introducing the
Spirit to His disciples, said "Ye know Him: for He
dwelleth with you and shall be in you" (John 14:17).
Just as it is possible for an unbeliever to know all about
the Lord Jesus and yet not know Him personally as
Lord and Saviour, so it is possible for you as a believer
to know all about the Holy Spirit and yet not know
Him as Companion and Friend. Paul prayed fervently
in his apostolic benediction, "The grace of the Lord
Jesus Christ, and the love of God, and the communion
of the Holy Ghost be with you all. Amen" (II Cor.
13:14). All such benedictions were originally suppli-
cations. This verse is really a personal prayer: "Oh
Father, let Thy love be manifested; Oh Lord Jesus, let
Thy grace be with us; Oh Holy Spirit, let Thy saints
enjoy much of Thy communion."

The Spirit of God loves us. He manifested His love
to us in bearing our insults, as we rejected His strivings
and pleadings to come to Christ (Hebrews 10:29—
"Despite"-insult). Would it not be strange indeed if

57

one of the Persons of the Godhead, Who loves, comforts and helps us to live the Christian life, should hold Himself aloof from sweet intercourse with the believer whom He indwells? He longs to commune with us; it is we who hinder the communion.

We can go to Him in every time of need. We can ask Him to help us to understand the Scriptures. We can ask Him to anoint us with fresh oil. We can ask Him to comfort us. We can ask Him to take of the treasures of Christ and reveal them unto us. We can ask Him to make Christ real to us. We can ask Him to glorify Christ in our lives. We can ask Him to reveal to us the mission field He has chosen for us. We can ask Him for guidance concerning every problem in our family life. We can ask Him to lead us to the person of His choice for marriage. We can ask Him how much money He wants us to give for a definite missionary cause. Even when we are at "wits-end corner" and the very bottom, as it were, seems to have suddenly fallen out of our lives, we can still ask Him to plan our future for us.

Many Bible teachers believe that it is not correct to pray to the Paraclete. I know from Scripture that in a general sense all prayer is addressed to God, the Father, in the Name of the Son, or through His merits, and energized by the power of the Spirit (Ephes. 3:14-21). But as Dr. John Owen reminds us, "We begin our prayers to God, the Father, and conclude them in the Name of Jesus Christ; yet the Son is no less invoked and worshipped in the beginning of our address than the Father, though He be peculiarly mentioned as Mediator in the close: not as Son to Himself, but as Mediator to God in Trinity. In the invocation of God, the Father, we invoke every Person, because we invoke the Father, as God, every Person being so." In that divine directory which is recorded by the apostle Paul in his Epistle to the Ephesians, chapter two, verse eighteen, for the benefit of the Church in all succeeding ages, this is fully declared. Our access and worship is said to be *to* the Father, *through* Christ, *by* the Spirit. "For through Him we both have access by one Spirit unto the Father."

Although the prayers in the New Testament are generally addressed to the Father, surely there is no harm in praying to the Son and the Spirit. I know of several hymn books of worship, where almost half the number are addressed to the Son and not the Father. There is just as much Scriptural authority to pray to the Spirit as there is to pray to the Son. Just as there are a few Scriptures where prayer is addressed to the Lord Jesus, so there are just a few where prayer is addressed to the Holy Spirit. For example, the Lord Jesus exhorts His disciples, "Pray ye, therefore, the Lord of the harvest, that He will send forth labourers into His harvest" (Matt. 9:38). In the Acts of the Apostles, we find that the Holy Spirit is the Lord of the harvest, and that He is the One Who calls and thrusts forth the labourers. "The Spirit of the Lord caught away Philip" (Acts 8:39). Paul invoked the Spirit for the believers at Thessalonica: "And the Lord direct your hearts into the love of God and into the patient waiting for Christ" (II Thess. 3:5).

The Moravians have left a rich legacy to the Church in some beautiful hymns invoking the Spirit, such as this:

> To Thee, God the Holy Ghost, we pray,
>   Who lead'st us in the Gospel way,
> Those precious gifts on us bestow,
>   Which from our Saviour's merits flow.

59

Thou heavenly Teacher, Thee we praise,
For Thy instruction, power and grace,
To love the Father, Who doth own
Us as His children in the Son.

Most gracious Comforter, we pray,
Oh lead us further every day:
Thy unction to us all impart,
Preserve and sanctify each heart!

Till we in heaven shall take our seat,
Instruct us often to repeat
"Abba", our Father; and to be
With Christ in union constantly.

Count Zinzendorf.

Bishop Spangenberg, John Wesley's first Moravian teacher, has written:

O Spirit of the Lord, all life is Thine;
Now fill Thy Church with life and power divine,
That many children may be born to Thee
And spread Thy knowledge like the boundless sea
To Christ's great praise.

In closing, may I give my own personal experience of the Spirit's ministry in my life. While I have known many renewings of the Holy Spirit since my conversion, two experiences will always live in my memory till my Father takes me Home to Glory. I was born again of the Spirit at the age of fourteen years, and immediately began to proclaim the glorious Gospel of the grace of God. It was six months later, however, at a Bible study in our assembly in Glasgow, that I made the startling discovery that the Holy Spirit is just as much a Person as is the Son of God. A dear brother had proved conclusively from John's Gospel that evening that the Holy Spirit was a divine Person Whom we, as believers, ought to know. I trembled with excitement in my seat until the meeting had finished. I rushed to my mother and my older brother and excitedly asked them if they knew this wonderful truth. They quietly replied that they did, and that I also should know it when I had a New Testament in my hands! It was hard for me to sleep that night. I had been born of the Spirit, sealed by the Spirit, indwelt by the Spirit, and introduced to the blessed Redeemer by Him, and yet during the first six months of my new life in Christ I did not know that the Holy Spirit was a Person! This was a revolutionary experience in my life. I immediately began to emphasize His personality and deity in all gatherings for believers where I had opportunity to speak. I zealously took to task any brother who, in his speech, inferred that the Spirit was not a Person.

Some years later I had another transforming experience. I began my ministry in Eastern Europe in my early twenties. God gave us revival in Riga, Latvia, which is now in Soviet Russia. The meetings there continued day and night as in the Welsh Revival. At four o'clock one morning I came out of the meeting to try to get an hour's sleep, when the Holy Spirit began to speak to me in my room. It was then and there that I entered into a personal fellowship with Him. For the first time in my Christian life I knew the Holy Spirit intimately as a Person. This experience, I believe, was a turning point in my ministry. Now think of this: I had received a direct supernatural call from the Holy Ghost in the little island of Stronsay in the Orkney group off the north coast of Scotland. There the Spirit spoke to me just as clearly and definitely as He spoke to Philip, (Acts 8:29), and told me to go and begin work among the Slavic races, beginning in the city of Riga. God had been using me as an evangelist and Bible teacher in

Great Britain, so that I had invitations for years ahead. Then suddenly the Spirit said to me, "Go to Riga." Without any farewell meeting, without any deputation work, and without any group behind me, I went alone, stepping out on the assurance of this unique call of the Lord of the Harvest. The call and leading was all in the atmosphere of the Acts, and yet I had still this glorious experience awaiting me. Between the two experiences of my first discovery that the Holy Spirit was a Person and my entering into an intimate communion with Him, I had from time to time been conscious of His guidance in my life. I knew His voice. Yet, on that early morning in Riga, I began a new life of constant, intimate communion with the Third Person of the Trinity.

It is the birthright privilege of every believer to enter into and maintain a life of conscious fellowship and communion with the divine Spirit.

Five

Power From on High

"They were to be baptized with the Holy Spirit, and receive such power and courage thereby as to bear a noble testimony for Christ".　　*John Gill*

"There can be no experience superior to or more wonderful than the baptism of the Spirit except to be in heaven itself".　　*Thomas Goodwin*

"Any impartation of the Holy Spirit is a baptism, and certainly, apart from Biblical phraseology, a filling with the Spirit may be called a baptism with the Spirit".　　*Dr. Hodge*

"We must withhold our consent from the inconsistent exegesis which would make the water baptism of the apostolic times still rigidly binding, but would relegate the baptism in the Spirit to a bygone dispensation. We hold indeed, that Pentecost was once for all, but equally that the appropriation of the Spirit by believers is always for all, and that the shutting up of certain great blessings of the Holy Ghost within that ideal realm called "the apostolic age", however convenient it may be as an escape from fancied difficulties, may be the means of robbing believers of some of their most precious covenant rights."   *A. J. Gordon*

AN ELECTRICITY BREAK-DOWN IN NORTH-eastern England recently trapped 20,000 miners underground in more than a hundred pits in County Durham and Northumberland. The break-down began with a blue flash in the £35 million South Stella Power Station, at Blaydon-on-Tyne. The break-down cost Britain millions of pounds sterling. Industry was stopped over a great area, including the whole of Tyneside's great shipbuilding and engineering works. Operations were delayed in some hospitals since they could not operate the X-Ray equipment as there was no power for three and one-half hours. One thousand three hundred workers were idle in one factory. In the busy intersections there were no traffic lights. Shops closed in the midst of a busy Christmas rush. The British Broadcasting Corporation transmitters were off the air for some hours. Wages were late for some workers as the computing machines stopped. Biscuits were burned at a South-Sheild's factory because the electric power-conveyers taking them from the gas-heated ovens stopped. And in the homes 400,000 consumers were cut off from the use of household electrical appliances.

The above incident is a striking parable of the condition of the Church of Jesus Christ today, as she is seeking to operate without the power of Pentecost. The primal need of the evangelical world is not for better machinery nor more gifted men, nor for prestige nor money, but for supernatural power. We all agree, to a certain extent, that this is the great need of the Church. Moreover we all agree that power comes from the Third Person of the Trinity. We all agree concerning His personality and His deity. Yet, when it comes to stating in clear definite terms His operations in the mystical body of Christ for spiritual power, we greatly differ. I believe that such disagreement among Fundamentalists not only brings confusion to young believers who are seeking power in their life and ministry, but it is also a hindrance to the Spirit Himself "breaking forth" in His mighty Majesty. How strange the fact that if a conference of Fundamentalists today were to gather in London, Stockholm, New York, or Sydney, to discuss "the Person and Work of the Son of God," they would all heartily agree; but if the theme was "The Person and Work of the Spirit of God," they would all heartily disagree. Moreover, the advocates of the various schools of thought concerning the Holy Spirit would, in many instances, refuse to have real heart-fellowship with each other. Some would go so far as to say that the others are propounding false doctrine.

The following are some of the view-points that would be brought forward; though not necessarily in the order mentioned here:

1st. You receive the Holy Ghost at the moment of your regeneration as the indwelling Guest.

"In Him you also, who have heard the Word of truth, the Gospel of your salvation, and have be-

lieved in Him, were sealed with the promised Holy
Spirit." (Eph. 1:13 R.V.)

2nd. You must receive the Baptism of power before
you can receive the Holy Spirit as the indwelling Guest.

"Did you receive the Holy Spirit when you believed?" (Acts. 19:2 R.V.)

3rd. Believers do not receive the Person of the Holy
Spirit at regeneration, but only the Spirit of Sonship.
The Spirit of Sonship is not the Holy Spirit Himself.

"If any man have not the Spirit of Christ, he is none
of His" (Rom. 8:9)

4th. Before one can receive the Spirit the elders of
the Church must lay their hands upon him.

"Then laid they their hands on them and they received the Holy Ghost." (Acts. 8:17)

5th. There is no such thing as the Baptism of Power.
There is only one baptism, which is the baptism of
being incorporated into the body of Christ.

"For by one Spirit are we all baptized into one
body, whether we be Jews or Gentiles, whether we
be bond or free; and have been all made to drink
in one Spirit" (I Cor. 12:13). It must be said, however, that the advocates of this viewpoint believe
that there is a scriptural experience of being "Filled
with the Spirit."

6th. There is "one baptism, but many fillings."
This is a phrase taken from the Scofield Bible. As
a footnote to the second chapter of Acts the following sentence appears: "The N. T. distinguishes between having the Spirit, which is true of all believers, and being filled with the Spirit, which is
the believer's privilege and duty. (cf. Acts 2:4 with
4:29-31; Eph. 1:13, 14 with 5:18)—'One baptism,
many fillings'."

67

This statement has been interpreted from two different standpoints: 1st. that the "baptism" refers to enduement of power for Christian service, followed by fresh infillings, as the need may arise. 2nd. That this "baptism" is that referred to in I Corinthians 12:13, when the believer is incorporated into the body of Christ, after which it is his privilege to seek renewals of the Spirit.

7th. The baptism referred to in I Corinthians 12:13 is identical with regeneration:

"When Paul declares in I Cor. 12:13, "For by one Spirit are we all baptized into one body," he is speaking of every believer having been quickened from the dead by the agency of the Holy Ghost, and thus made a member of Christ's mystical body. This is the Pauline way of stating the being born again of John 3:7" (John McNeil of Australia).

8th. One receives "everything" at conversion, and thus to teach a deeper work of the Spirit is unscriptural.

"And of His fulness have all we received, and grace for grace". (John 1:16. cf. Col. 2:10)

9th. There is only one crisis, and that is the crisis of regeneration.

"Ye must be born again". (John 3:7)

The secret of success in the Christian life is progressive sanctification. "But grow in grace, and in the knowledge of our Lord and Saviour Jesus Christ" (II Peter 3:18).

10th. The Baptism with (or in) the Spirit is for power for Christian service only.

Dr. Torrey says "The Baptism with the Holy Spirit is not primarily for the purpose of making us individually holy. Please note carefully my words and grasp exactly what I say. I do not say that it is not the work of the Holy Spirit to make us holy, for it is His work to make us holy, and it is only through His work that any one of us can become holy. I do say, however, that it is not the primary purpose of the Baptism with the Holy Spirit to make us holy. *The primary purpose of the Baptism with the Holy Spirit is to equip us and fit us for service . . . .*

"Neither is it the primary purpose of the Baptism with the Holy Spirit to make us personally happy. Note again carefully what I say. I do not say that the Baptism with the Spirit will not make us happy, if we receive it. I have never known anyone yet who was 'baptized with the Holy Spirit' into whose heart a new and more wonderful joy did not come, but I am saying that *this is not the primary purpose of the Baptism with the Holy Spirit.* The primary purpose of the Baptism with the Holy Spirit is not to make us happy but to make us useful for God. I am glad that this is so, for while ecstasies are all right in their place, and while I know something about them in my own experience, yet in a world such as you and I live in, where there is this awful tide of men, women, and children sweeping on unsaved to a hopeless eternity, I would rather go my entire life through without one single touch of ecstasy or rapture and have power to do my part to stem this awful tide and save at least some, than to have indescribable raptures every day of my life and have no power to save the lost."

11th. *The Baptism of power is for inward sanctification alone.*

"And God, which knoweth the hearts, bare them witness, giving them the Holy Ghost, even as He did unto us; and put no difference between us and them, purifying their hearts by faith." (Acts 15: 8,9)

12th. *There are many baptisms for power in the Christian life.*

Charles Finney says:

"Every step of progress in the Christian life is taken by a fresh and fuller appropriation of Christ by faith, a fuller baptism of the Holy Spirit" . . . . "As we are more and more emptied of all self-dependence, and as by faith we secure deeper and deeper baptisms of the Holy Ghost, and put on the Lord Jesus Christ more thoroughly, by just so much faster do we grow in the favour of God. . . . You must pray in faith for the Holy Spirit. At every forward step in your progress you must have a fresh anointing of the Holy Spirit through faith." Mr. Finney speaks again and again in his story of his evangelistic labors of receiving many baptisms of power. So far as I know, Mr. Finney, William Booth, and James Caughey (who won Booth for Christ), are the only exponents of this thought.

13th. The *initial evidence* of being baptized with the Spirit *is supernaturally speaking in "tongues."*

"And they were all filled with the Holy Ghost, and began to speak with other tongues, as the Spirit gave them utterance." (Acts. 2:4)

The following is the testimony of Pastor Lewi Pethrus, pastor of the largest evangelical church in Europe. (Mr. Pethrus received a Doctorate from Wheaton College, Illinois.)

"I was a preacher from 1902, but I was in very dry surroundings; I would not condemn any church, but it was dry around me, and I was often dry too, and my spiritual life went down more and

more. One day I was really a backslider. The
people around me did not know, but I knew, and
God knew, and God waked me up and I started to
pray. Sometimes I prayed night and day. Then
before Christmas 1905 I had a wonderful meeting
with God, and He cleansed my soul and my heart
once more. I got two books in my hands; one was
the story of Charles Finney's life, and the other
was a book by R. A. G. Goreham about the two-
fold life. It was about this: that you could not
only be converted and born again, but you could
be baptized in the Holy Spirit. I was praying and
longing for it, but first thought that this was a
blessing for Charles Finney—he was a great man,
and a great instrument that God used—but it is
not for me: and I heard about Moody and men
that God had mightily used, and I thought it was
for them, but not for me. But one day I saw clearly
that it was for me. It is for us all, hallelujah! . . . .
After a revival meeting one night I went on my
knees in my own room and there the blessed Spirit
filled this empty place in my heart. Later I started
to pray, and as I did so, I began to speak in
tongues. That evening I could not preach. I could
not read. I could not do anything. I could only
speak in tongues."

The above is the experience that many teach is necessary before one can claim the "baptism of the Spirit."

14th. The "Baptism" and the "Filling" are synony-
mous.

"Ye shall be baptized with the Holy Ghost not
many days hence." (Acts. 1:5)

"And they were all filled with the Holy Ghost."
(Acts. 2:4)

It seems that the evangelical writers of the past

71

generations chiefly used the term "a baptism of power."
(Although an exception may be mentioned in John
Goodwin, the old Puritan, when preaching in Colman
Street, London, in 1620, gave a series of addresses
entitled "A Being Filled With the Spirit," which would
fill a modern book of a thousand pages!) I believe that
it is only in modern times, because of the phenomenal
growth of the "Pentecostal Movement" that many
writers and teachers have begun to use exclusively the
word "fulness," hoping thereby to avoid the association
of "tongues" with the ministry of the Spirit. The chang-
ing of terms in this respect, however, is not altogether
logical in the light of Acts. 2:4; "And they were all
filled with the Holy Ghost and began to speak with
other tongues as the Spirit gave them utterance."

If the above-mentioned teachings could be divided
logically into two schools of evangelical faith, such as
Arminian and Calvinistic, it would simplify matters
considerably. It is not, however, as easy as that, for
we find teachers and preachers of the same denomina-
tion holding different and widely-varying views concerning the operation of the Spirit.

We cannot doubt the sincerity and the maturity of
the different men today who hold these various lines
of thought. I will gladly go to any brother who holds
a view different from my own, and humbly and re-
spectfully seek a unity of understanding through the
Word of God. I will not argue over the Person and
work of the Holy Spirit, *for He is too precious and holy
for argument. We either know Him or we do not know
Him* in a real vital way. "But ye know Him; for He
dwelleth with you, and shall be in you," the Saviour
prophesied. (John 14:17). It is interesting to notice
that men of God who use different expressions describe
the same experience with the Spirit in their own lives.

Mr. Finney speaks of his "initial Baptism" in the following way: "As I went in and shut the door after me, it seemed as if I met the Lord Jesus Christ face to face. . . . He said nothing, but looked at me in such a manner as to break me right down at His feet. I wept aloud like a child, and made such confessions as I could with my choked utterance. . . . As I turned and was about to take a seat by the fire, *I received a mighty baptism of the Holy Ghost.* . . . No words can express the wonderful love which was shed abroad in my heart. I wept with joy and love."

Mr. Moody's testimony is given by Dr. R. A. Torrey. Although D. L. Moody used both terms, "Baptism," and "Filling," Dr. Torrey uses the word "Baptism" in referring to the experience of Mr. Moody, in his book, "Why God Used D. L. Moody":

"The seventh thing that was the secret why God used D. L. Moody was that he had a very definite enduement with power from on high, a very clear and definite 'Baptism with the Holy Ghost'; he had no doubt about it. In his early days he was a great hustler; he had a tremendous desire to do something, but he had no real power. He worked very largely in the energy of the flesh. But there were two humble "Free Methodist" women who used to come over to his meetings in the Y.M.C.A. One was 'Auntie Cook' and the other Mrs. Snow (I think her name was not Snow at that time). These two women would come to Mr. Moody at the close of his meetings and say: 'We are praying for you.' Finally, Mr. Moody became somewhat nettled and said to them one night: 'Why are you praying for me? Why don't you pray for the unsaved?' They replied, 'We are praying that you may get the power.' Mr. Moody did not know what they meant, but he got to thinking about it, and then went to those women and said: 'I wish you would tell me what you mean' and they told him about the definite Baptism with the Holy Ghost. Then he asked that he might pray *with* them and not they merely pray for him.

"Auntie Cook once told me of the intense fervour with which Mr. Moody prayed on that occasion. She told me in words that I scarcely dare repeat, though I have never forgotten them. And he not only prayed with them, but he also prayed alone. Not long after, one day on his way to England, he was walking up Wall Street in New York (Mr. Moody very seldom told this and I almost hesitate to tell it) and in the midst of the bustle and hurry of that city, his prayer was answered: the power of God fell upon him as he walked up the street and he had to hurry off to the house of a friend and ask that he might have a room by himself, and in that room he stayed alone for hours; and the Holy Ghost came upon him, filling his soul with such joy that at last he had to ask God to withhold His hand, lest he die on the spot from very joy. He went out from that place with the power of the Holy Ghost upon him, and when he got to London (for a quiet visit. J.A.S.) the power of God wrought through him mightily in North London and hundreds were added to the Church, and that was what led to his being invited over for the wonderful campaign that followed in later years."

The late Dr. Charles Inwood of the Keswick Convention Movement describes his experience as "the Fulness": *

"May I, in all humility, be permitted to give a

*Dr. Inwood also used the term "Baptism."

testimony. It may help somebody. In my own case,
God led me definitely early one Friday morning
simply as a little child, to trust Him for this precious gift, the fulness of the Spirit. By simple faith,
naked faith, I took the gift, but I was not conscious of receiving anything. All through that day
there seemed even a greater dryness and dulness
in my soul—no new pulsations, no new sense of the
presence of God. How often during the day the
devil came and said: 'You have trusted God to fill
you with the Spirit; see how you feel! Why you do
not feel that you have as much of God in you now as
last week!' And that was true. Friday went and Saturday came, and it seemed a very long day; there
was the same dryness and the absence of the presence of God, and all during Saturday the tempter
still more powerfully assailed my faith in God, but I
held on to God—to His promise; to His unchanging
faithfulness to His own Word. It is always a thousand times better to trust in the faithfulness of God
than in the fitfulness of one's poor senses. Sunday
came; Sunday morning just as dry as ever; and
during that Sunday morning service, during the
proclamation of the message—for, praise God, He
can bless the soul of the speaker even while speaking the message in the Master's name; if He did
not I do not know what some of us would do—but
that morning, as I was speaking His message to the
people, there came silently stealing into my heart
a strange new sense of ease and rest and peace.
That is how it began; and then it deepened hour by
hour during the day, deepened in the service in the
evening, and in the after-meeting it seemed to
culminate in one great tidal wave of the glory of
God, that swelled and submerged and interpene-

75

trated, and broke me down in silent, holy adoration
in God's presence. God had fulfilled His promise on
the Friday morning, but He wanted to test the faith
of his servant, and God sent that sweet, sacred,
never-to-be-forgotten sense of His presence at the
earliest moment that it was good for His yielded,
obedient, trusting child."

In connection with the foregoing statements, I may
add that personally I use the terms "Baptism" and
"Fulness" interchangeably, as I believe the Scriptures
warrant us to do so.

I believe there are two spiritual baptisms, apart from
the ordinance of water baptism; the baptism by the
Spirit into the body of Christ, and the baptism by Christ
with power from on high. Many Bible expositors infer
from Paul's statement in Ephesians 4:5: "One Lord,
one faith, one baptism," that it is unscriptural to say
that there is more than one baptism, and hence, one
must not use the term "baptism of power." These same
writers and teachers, in order to prove that there is only
one baptism spoken of in the New Testament, teach
that the "baptism" spoken of in Romans 6:3,4 and
Colossians 2:12 is the one and same baptism of the
Spirit into the body of Christ. By teaching this, they
would explain away water baptism. Paul could not
have expounded a precious truth concerning the believer's death, burial, and resurrection with Christ and
the walk in newness of life if there had been no ordinance of water baptism.

Pentecost marked the beginning or formation of a
new body or organism which is designated by Paul,
"The Church, which is His body." Having been incorporated into Christ by the New Birth (II Cor. 5:17),
we are then incorporated into His mystical, supernatural
body by the Spirit's baptism.

"For as the body is one, and hath many members, and all the members of that one body, being many are one body: so also is Christ. For by one Spirit are we all baptized into one body." (I Cor. 12:12,13).

By this baptism we are united to Christ the Head and united to each member of the body. This supernatural body is composed of all regenerated people, who have believed in the Lord Jesus Christ, both Jew and Gentile, out of all nations and denominations, blessed with all spiritual blessings in the heavenlies in Christ, sealed by the Spirit individually, and baptized by the Spirit collectively.

"And He is the head of the body, the Church" (Col. 1:18).

"And not holding the Head, from which all the body by joints and bands having nourishment ministered and knit together, increaseth with the increase of God" (Col. 2:19).

"And gave Him to be the head over all things to the Church" (Eph. 1:22).

"There is one body, and one Spirit" (Eph. 4:4).

"Now ye are the body of Christ, and members in particular" (I Cor. 12:27).

I was brought up with a group of believers who rejoice in this truth possibly more than any company of saints. They hold to this doctrine as a fundamental feature of the Christian life, so that I have revelled in the reality of the union of the body of Christ with the Head all my entire Christian experience. The Upper Room was the Spirit's baptistry, where the believers were baptized by the Holy Spirit into one body.

> Lord Jesus, are we one with Thee?
> Oh height, Oh depth, of love!
> Thou one with us on Calvary,
> We one with Thee above.

Ascended now, in glory bright,
  Head of the Church Thou art;
No life nor death, nor depth nor height
  Thy saints in Thee can part.

Oh teach us, Lord, to know and own
  This wondrous mystery,
That Thou in heaven with us art one,
  And we are one with Thee.

J. G. Deck

The leaders of the evangelical churches in Hungary agree that it was my preaching of this glorious doctrine that brought revival to their land some twenty years ago. The expounding of this truth to a believer's heart can revolutionize his entire Christian life and walk. Oh that saints everywhere would express in these dark needy days the unity of the body of Christ into which we have all been baptized by the Holy Spirit! The unity is there; it is for us to recognize and express it.

The Baptism with (Gr. en—"in") the Spirit as promised in Acts 1:5 is, however, distinct from the Baptism of I Corinthians 12:13. In order that the young believer may study the subject for himself, I am presenting all the Scriptures in the Gospels and in the first chapter of the Acts which speak of this baptism before Pentecost.

"He shall baptize you with the Holy Ghost" (Matt. 3:11).

"He shall baptize you with the Holy Ghost" (Mark 1:8).

"He shall baptize you with the Holy Ghost" (Luke 3:16).

"The same is he which baptizeth you with the Holy Ghost" (John 1:33).

"For John truly baptized with water; but ye shall be baptized with the Holy Ghost, not many days hence" (Acts. 1:5).

78

If a young babe in Christ in a village in Siberia had only the Four Gospels and the Acts of the Apostles in his possession, he could come to no other conclusion than that the promise of John the Baptist and of the Son of God was nothing less than a baptism of power for Christian witness. He would be led of the Spirit to read the following words in the last chapter of Luke's Gospel:

"And that repentance and remission of sins should be preached in His name among all nations, beginning at Jerusalem. And ye are witnesses of these things. And behold, I send the promise of my Father upon you: but tarry ye in the city of Jerusalem, until ye be endued with power from on high" (Luke 24:47-49).

As a hungry soul, he would continue to read Luke's narrative in the first chapter of the Acts concerning the charge and promise of the risen Lord.

"And, being assembled together with them, commanded them that they should not depart from Jerusalem, but wait for the promise of the Father, which, saith He, ye have heard of me. For John truly baptized with water, but ye shall be baptized with the Holy Ghost not many days hence. . . . Ye shall receive power, after that the Holy Ghost is come upon you: and ye shall be witnesses unto me. . ." (Acts. 1:8).

Surely this isolated young convert would not be led from these Scriptures to think of the baptism into the body of Christ, but rather a baptism of power.

The reader will notice that the Lord Jesus refers to the prophesy of John the Baptist when He says "For John truly baptized with water; but ye shall be baptized with the Holy Ghost." Why does the risen Saviour link up the two baptisms? Was it not to remind them of John's prophesy?

"There cometh one mightier than I after me, the

latchet of whose shoes I am not worthy to stoop down and unloose. I indeed have baptized you with water: but He shall baptize you with the Holy Ghost" (Mark. 1:7-8).

What did the Forerunner mean by this statement? Surely it is clear and so simple that the youngest child can understand: "I want to tell you of a greater Baptizer and a greater baptism than that of water. I am baptizing you in this water, but the Son of God will baptize you in the Spirit." If there were any doubt left in our minds that this baptism is one of power for witness, it would soon be dispelled by the striking similarity of the language used by our Lord:

"I send the promise of the Father UPON YOU."

"Ye shall receive power after that the Holy Ghost is come UPON YOU."

On the day of Pentecost the disciples received the fulfilment of the "promise of the Father" when the ascended Lord poured out His Spirit upon them.

"Being therefore lifted high by the mighty hand of God, He has received from the Father the *promised Holy Ghost*, and has poured out this which ye see and hear" (Acts. 2:33 Weymouth).

The miracle of Pentecost was the miracle of transformed lives. The disciples were robed with supernatural power. This met their desperate need. Theirs was an impossible task. Who would believe the fantastic story that the carpenter's son, who died such an ignoble death as a criminal on a felon's gibbet was none other than the risen Son of God? All the powers of hell were against them. They faced a hostile religious world. They faced an overpowering opposition from the heathen world. From the human viewpoint, they were doomed at the very beginning to fail in their mission. The coming of the Holy Spirit changed everything.

80

From their being incompetent, demoralized, powerless, and weak disciples they became effective, dynamic, and aggressive through the endowment of the Spirit, by the baptizing work of the Son. Look at Peter for example. Before Pentecost he warmed his hands at the world's fire; after Pentecost he warmed three thousand hearts with the preaching of the Word. Before Pentecost, he denied his Lord before a young peasant girl; after Pentecost he courageously and boldly faced the murderers of the Lord Jesus and charged them with the death of his blessed Saviour. Before Pentecost he denied the Lord three times; after Pentecost he was given one thousand souls for each time he denied him!

Pentecost is always associated with power. The subsequent reading of the Book of Acts reveals it to be a pageantry of power. You can write the one word "POWER" over every chapter and over every incident. "Ye shall receive POWER after that the Holy Ghost is come upon you." The baptism in the Holy Ghost was the authentic touch of God upon their lives. The Church in its first twenty-five years of existence accomplished more than at any other time in the history of Christianity.

I have read many books on the ministry of the Holy Spirit in which it was dogmatically stated that the promised baptism, predicted by John the Baptist and by our Lord, i.e., "the promise of the Father" has nothing whatever to do with power for Christian witness. This seems incredible. One is startled more when he realizes that such a statement comes from men of deep spiritual maturity.

As a young convert I respected my elders in their teaching that the baptism mentioned by John the Baptist was fulfilled in the incorporation of the believers into the body of Christ, according to I Corinthians 12:13. I accepted their teaching, as these men were spiritual, safe, and sane Bible scholars. They had an unequalled comprehensive grasp of the contents of the Word from Genesis to Revelation, which has enabled me to maintain a balanced Christian life.

Yet, as I continued to study the Word for myself on my knees, I was astounded to see that my conclusions on this matter differed from theirs. This pained me considerably, as I held these teachers and writers in high esteem. My seeking of the truth from the Word for myself arose from my desperate need of spiritual power in witnessing to my new-found Lord. More and more the scriptures quoted above encouraged me to believe that there was a mighty spiritual experience awaiting me which could be called "A baptism of power" or "the fulness of the Holy Ghost." God met my need and heart hunger in a very blessed way, for which I praise Him. After thirty years, without the bias of any particular Bible school or theological seminary background to color my thinking, it is still my definite conviction that "the promise of the Father" is a baptism of supernatural power.

Although I believe and preach the Spirit's baptism into the body of Christ, as one of the most vital truths of the Christian life, I do recognize that I Corinthians 12:13 is the only verse in the Bible that speaks of this baptizing work of the Spirit. Paul, in I Corinthians 12, is not expounding the Spirit's baptism to the Corinthian believers, but rather the unity of the various gifts in the body of Christ. In order to explain this unity, Paul refers them to this baptism. "A man's body is all one, though it has a number of different organs; and all this multitude of organs goes to make up one body; so it is with Christ. We too, all of us, have been baptized into a single body by the power of a single Spirit, Jews and

Greeks, slaves and freemen alike; we have all been given drink at a single source, the one Spirit" (Knox translation). Or as the Cambridge Greek New Testament renders the verse: "For by one Spirit (literally, in one Spirit, i.e., in virtue of His operation) are all we baptized into one body, whether we be Jews or Gentiles, whether we be bond or free; and have all been made to drink in one Spirit."

Of course, there are some allusions in the New Testament to this blessed fact, such as: "At that day (Pentecost) ye shall know that I am in my Father and ye in me, and I in you" (John 14:20).

"I am the vine; ye are the branches" (John 15:5).

"Upon this rock I will build my church" (Matt. 16: 18).

Also in the high-priestly prayer of our Lord in John, chapter seventeen, the spiritual eye can see in embryo the formation of the Body, when all believers would be united to the Head and to each other. We see also in Paul's epistles how he gloried in the reality of this blessed truth. To the apostle, it was one of the fundamental features of the Christian life.

To sum up our consideration: I Corinthians 12:13 is the baptizing work of the Spirit, incorporating believers into the body of Christ, while Acts. 1:5 is the baptizing work of the Son of God into the element of the Spirit.

The Baptism of the Spirit in I Corinthians 12:13 is an operation of the Spirit which takes place at regeneration, whether the believing soul is conscious of it or not; whereas the baptism of the Son of God as promised in Acts. 1:5 is a conscious experience which takes place in a believer's life when he meets God's conditions. J. Brainerd Taylor, Handley Moule, Andrew Murray, A. B. Simpson, A. J. Gordon, A. T. Pierson, Evan Roberts, and hosts of others have left a legacy to the Church in their testimonies of such a never-to-be-forgotten experience in their lives, when the Holy Ghost invaded their entire being and took control. There are thousands of little-known men and women also who can testify to a definite crisis in their Christian life, when they were "Empowered from on high." Who could come into contact with these precious souls and not recognize that there was something different about them from the ordinary type of Christian!

My friend, Dr. F. J. Miles, who, himself, uses the word "Fulness," in his book, "The Greatest Unused Power in the World," has this to say in closing a very valuable contribution to the study of the ministry of the Holy Spirit:

"I desire it to be clearly understood that nothing in my books in general and in this one in particular is to be construed as being in opposition to what is usually referred to as a second blessing. In the experience of most Christians the complete 'enthronement of Christ,' I Peter 3:15; the 'full surrender' of Romans 12:1 and 2; 6:11, etc.; 'the fulness of the Spirit' of Ephesians 5:18, Romans 8:1-4; 'entire sanctification' of I Thessalonians 5:23,24; 'perfect love' of Matthew 5:48; I John 4:16-19; Romans 13:9-10; Christ's New Commandment; and the like; being manifold expressions describing the life in which we are to be 'more than conquerors through Him who loved us' (Romans 8:37, does come as a *second* blessing. But this is not because God has not made full provision at the first, but because we lack knowledge and instruction at our conversion. Potentially, it is all there; we only come into possession when we are taught, know and submit to the truth. It was my privilege at my conversion to be in touch with 'The Grubb Party' (a Bible-teaching Evangelistic party of the Keswick Convention school of thought. Ed.), and I have never known any other teaching than that of full surrender to the Spirit of Christ and its ever-developing enrichment and blessedness. I could only wish that all our preachers were equally teachers of this glorious truth, so that for new converts there might be no long wilderness wanderings, but an immediate entrance into Canaan."

Let us pray with D. L. Moody:

"Our Heavenly Father, we come to wait on Thee for the gift of Thy Holy Spirit for service. Oh God, give us the Spirit. Empty us of self and self-seeking. Oh God, bring us down in the dust before Thee, so that we may be filled with the Holy Ghost, so that we may have power with God and with man! Oh Thou God of Elijah, we pray that a double portion of Thy Spirit may come upon us today, that we may be anointed for the work Thou hast for us to do; we know that we have but a little while to stay here!

"Oh, God, help us to bear fruit while we live! May we no longer be toiling day after day and month after month, and seeing no fruit. Oh Jesus, Master, Thou hast gone up on high; Thou hast led captivity captive; Thou art at the right hand of God, and Thou hast power.

"O, give us power; Thou canst give us a fresh anointing. We pray that Thou wilt do it today. We pray that Thou wilt breathe upon us as a breath from heaven. Grant that we may know what it is to have the Holy Ghost resting upon us for service. . . . We ask it all in the Name and for the sake of Thy beloved Son." Amen!

Six

Baptism of Power

"The day of Pentecost was a pattern day; all the days of this dispensation should have been like it, or should have exceeded it. But, alas, the Church has fallen down to the state in which it was before this blessing had been bestowed, and it is necessary for us to ask Christ to begin over again. We, of course, in respect and knowledge—intellectual knowledge of spiritual things—are far in advance of the point where the disciples were before Pentecost. But it should be borne in mind, that when truths have once been fully revealed and been made a part of orthodoxy, the holding of them does not necessarily imply an operation of the Spirit of God. We deceive ourselves, doubtless, in this way, imagining that, because we have the whole Scripture, and are conversant with all its great truths, the Spirit of God is necessarily working in us. We need a Baptism of the Spirit as much as the apostles did at the time of Christ's resurrection; we need that the unsearchable riches of Christ should be revealed to us more copiously than they were to Isaiah in the temple".   *George Bowen*

T HE GREATEST WITNESS TO THE VERACITY
of the truth of enduement with power is the exhibition of this power in the lives of men and women,
whether famous or unknown. "An ounce of experience
is worth a ton of theory" says an old proverb. As an
open-air preacher I have always found, in street meetings or in public parks, that the unsaved will listen with
greater intensity to the simple witness of an ordinary
brother describing his Damascus Road experience, than
to the most brilliant sermon of a mighty preacher. The
first question that comes to the mind of the listeners
when hearing a doctrine expounded is, "Does it work
out in every-day life?" The transformed, dynamic, holy
lives of the new-born in Christ do more to convince
men of the reality of the Gospel, than all the sermons
ever preached, or the books ever written, on the evidences of Christianity. The greatest evidence of the new
birth is a young convert standing on his two feet witnessing for Christ. And the greatest evidence of the
baptism of power from on high is one insignificant life
radiating the glory of the Lord and supernaturally
winning souls for Christ.

As a child in Scotland, I was surrounded by an over-whelming cloud of witnesses to the supernatural power of God, both in the history of evangelical life and in my own personal contacts. I heard of the mighty exploits of the Covenanters. I went to sleep at night dreaming of the prophetic insight and miracles of Michael Peden. I heard in the Sunday School of the saintliness of the Bonar brothers and of Murray McCheyne. At home I heard the reading of the letters of the prisoner of the Lord, Samuel Rutherford, in which he told of his deep, intimate love-life with the Son of God. I read of Benjamin Abbott, who was converted late in life, and who was so illiterate that he preached on "the oyster man," mis-reading the words "austere man" in Luke 19:21; how he preached with such power and unction that thousands were added to the Lord through his ministry.

I saw everywhere the evidences of the fruit of the Moody and Sankey evangelistic campaigns. All around me were Gospel agencies which were established through the revival of their time. There was the Glasgow Evangelistic Association with its Gospel Halls filled with thousands of praising saints. There was the Glasgow Bible Training Institute, where by friend Dr. D. M. McIntyre (Andrew Bonar's son-in-law) was the beloved principal. This institute was sending out young people to the ends of the earth as missionaries, and training pastors and evangelists for Great Britain. There was the St. George's Cross Tabernacle of which Pastor Findlay was the founder and pastor. Here was a Bible-teaching and missionary centre for the whole of Scotland, which sent forth and supported missionaries around the world. I heard from Pastor Findlay's own lips of the night when, in a small meeting of one thousand young men, one hundred accepted Christ as Lord and Saviour when Mr. Moody gave the invitation.

Pastor Findlay was among them. He told how, without exception, every one of these one hundred young men became stalwarts for Christ.

As I began to travel all through the British Isles, the same story repeated itself, of the lasting fruit of the ministry of these two men of God. The ministry of Torrey, Chapman and Alexander was, in one sense, the continuance of the blessing begun in Britain during Mr. Moody's time. I met Christians of all walks of life, from noblemen to cottagers, who owed, humanly speaking, their conversion to Mr. Moody. It is not too much to say that almost every evangelical agency at home and abroad in those days owed a mighty debt to the work of God through the American evangelist. Hundreds of thousands of pounds were given for the Lord's work, many selling their property and giving the money for the spread of the Gospel. Hundreds of young men and women gave themselves to missionary service. There was little lack of money or labourers in those days. As a young convert, I looked upon all this lasting fruit of the ministry of this servant of God, and I cried to God to show me the secret of Mr. Moody's power. Here was a man with little learning, whose English grammar was a source of offence to refined ears, winning the highest in society and the highest intellectuals to Christ. Surely his was a supernatural power with God and man.

At the same time I was challenged through the ministry of my spiritual father, Mr. Tom Rea of Belfast, Northern Ireland. Though he had not the privilege of theological training, the Lord sent him forth to labour among the dear Roman Catholics in the south of Ireland. There he lost his health as the result of injuries received at the hands of those whom he had gone to bless, and was forced to leave his mission field. He came to labour as an evangelist in Scotland. I had heard many mighty

91

preachers, but the moment I heard Mr. Tom Rea for the first time, I knew I could no longer resist the wooings of the Spirit of God to come to Christ. In later years, as I laboured with him, I would know him in terrible bodily weakness, literally to depend upon God to help him to reach the platform without collapsing. He would preach with such indescribable power that the congregation could not leave the building; the powers of the unseen world were manifested and the hush of eternity was upon the gathering. Sinners trembled under the mighty convicting power of the Holy Spirit as "hell had enlarged herself and opened her mouth without measure" (Isa. 5:14). Many times the saints could not sleep because they had caught a vision of the glories of heaven in the meeting. It was evident that the power of Mr. Rea was something apart from himself, since he knew no eloquence and grandeur in his preaching.

One of the most extraordinary lives that blessed and challenged my young Christian life was that of a young girl in my city of Glasgow, who came to the Lord about the same time as I. Although this young lady went to glory at about the age of twenty-two, she left behind her one of the most fragrant Christlike testimonies I have ever known. She was born into a working class home, even as I had been. Soon after her conversion she dedicated her life for foreign missionary work, and set herself to prepare for the task. Her one thought, one desire, one object in life was Christ; she was filled with Christ. Her one delight was to talk of the One she loved so well, so that when believers left her presence they felt the glory of the Lord in their own souls. In the University where she studied, it was even as in the church, her simple testimony was backed by the power of the Holy Spirit of God. Yet, perhaps it was her prayer life which was her greatest testimony for the Lord. She kept a prayer diary over which she prayed, and in which she recorded marvellous answers to her prayers, both for individuals whom she knew at home, and for missionaries with their needs on the foreign field.

Thus it was that when God was pleased to call my young friend home at an early age, many thousands of us cried like David of old: "How are the mighty fallen in the midst of the battle!" Lonely missionaries in far-off places wept when they heard the news. A large crowd attended her funeral. An unsaved grave-digger told me that in all his experience he had never felt the mighty power of God in such a way as at the burial of this young lady. She had not been a preacher, nor a singer, nor anyone famous, but rather just an ordinary believer in the Lord Jesus who had given her life to be filled with Him. Yet, to my mind, her lone testimony produced greater and more far-reaching results than the combined witness of hundreds of believers around her. Hers was the supernatural life in the Spirit which encouraged my own soul at that time.

Later in my Christian life, it was my privilege to know and to labour with Mrs. Catherine Booth-Clibborn* (La Marechale). I saw the mighty effects of her long and varied ministry, which covered some seventy years in aggressive evangelism. I was in the studio of the British Broadcasting Corporation in London when she spoke to the British Empire on the occasion of her ninetieth birthday, and later on the platform with her at a great public meeting held in her honour in the Central Hall, Westminster. At that time cables and letters poured in from all parts of the globe, from royalty and common people alike. As I read some of them I was deeply moved to think of so many who had been won to

*Eldest daughter of the founders of the Salvation Army.

Christ by the old soldier of the Cross down the years. After the meeting in Westminster, hundreds crowded around her to tell of some particular meeting or occasion in which they had found Christ through her ministry, whether in Australia, Europe, or North America.

As it was in the case of Mr. Rea, I have known Mrs. Booth-Clibborn to receive such an anointing of the Spirit, while thousands were awaiting her message, and when it seemed an utter impossibility for her to speak even a few words, that she was enabled to go to the platform and preach for an hour in mighty soul-saving power. And this in her ninety-second year!

Time would fail me to tell of the influence of the lives and ministry of men like W. P. Nicholson and Jock Troop, as well as many others. In them I saw first-hand this mighty baptism of power manifesting itself in supernatural revival in Ulster and Scotland. One could go on indefinitely telling of ordinary, as well as famous people, who received the Spirit's enduement of power. One thing is certain, it was impossible to be long in the presence of these dear ones, without knowing that they were different from the ordinary type of Christian. Whenever I have met these people, I have been driven to my knees to thank God for every remembrance of them, and to ask that I, too, may be led into a fuller, richer and deeper experience of His grace and power. Every one of the above-mentioned people had a definite crisis after regeneration, when they were "baptized" or "filled" with the Holy Ghost.

In closing, I would mention one more incident which blessed my soul, and which I pray may bless yours:

One day in Texas, tired and weary after many months of missionary deputation work, I asked the Lord fervently to somehow, in an unusual way, give us a warm missionary gathering in the evening. I had been ministering in so many cold fundamental churches, that I longed for a fresh touch from God. I asked my hostess during the evening meal how many believers in her church were filled with the Holy Spirit. She was astonished at my question. She exclaimed, "Mr. Stewart, I would have you know that ours is a fundamental church! You have to be born again to be a member of our assembly."

"I did not ask you how many were born again; I asked how many were filled with the Spirit."

There was no answer, but a discreet silence rested over us during the remainder of the meal. Evidently the dear sister was disturbed in her own mind, and had been thinking the question over, for as we walked to church afterwards, she suddenly stopped in the street and said, "Preacher, I think I know what you mean! I think we have one member of our church filled with the Holy Ghost."

I asked her to kindly describe that one to me. She said he was an old Swedish grandfather, and that when he prayed, alternating between Swedish and broken English, the whole atmosphere of the church was strangely warmed. I told her that this man certainly had the symptoms of the fulness! I asked the Lord that night to please move the pastor to call on this dear brother to pray. I was desperate. I soon discovered that this was going to be another cold, dead missionary meeting, unless something happened. It was a Bible-believing church, but one that held the doctrine of the Word with coldness of heart. I dreaded the service, for surely there is nothing so wearing to the nerves, and so damaging to the soul, as to plead for the lost on the mission field in a cold, dead spiritual atmosphere. I cried again to the Lord, and He heard my prayer, for when the pastor called on someone to pray, the old

Swedish gentleman stood up. I cannot tell you to this day what he said in his prayer because I was transported to glory! The prayer had finished and the pastor had announced that I would speak, and still I sat in the presence of my Lord. The pastor had to speak to me the second time before I came to earth again! Needless to say, it was a glorious, heart-warming missionary meeting that evening. After the service I walked the streets saying in my heart, "Oh God, if we could only have one brother or sister in every evangelical church in North America, so filled with the Holy Ghost, we would soon have revival."

Oh, dear brother and sister, I believe that this is the most important subject in the book. This is a chapter that could challenge and revolutionize your entire Christian life. As we have already said in the previous chapter, we will not stay for one second to argue with you concerning the terminology of the mighty ministry of the Spirit, but that we will gladly go into the secret place with any of you and kneel as brother and friend and cry with you for this supernatural power for our life and ministry. I am convinced that many have the right terminology who have no experience; while many have a definite experience who describe it with the wrong terminology. This is a theme that humbles every one of us to the dust before God. Who are we that we should be filled with the Holy Spirit of God? Who are we that the Lord Jesus should condescend to baptize us with His power?

Lord, Thou knowest all the hunger
    Of the heart that seeks Thee now;
How my soul hath long been craving
    What Thou only canst bestow.

    Seeking now, seeking now,
    Let Thy Spirit meet me now.

Failure in my walk and witness,
    Failure in my work I see;
Fruitless toil, un-Christlike living,
    Calling forth no praise to Thee.

Now to Thee my soul confesses
    All its failure, all its sin;
All the pride, the self-contentment,
    All the "secret faults" within.

Save me from myself, my Father,
    From each subtle form of pride;
Lead me now with Christ to Calvary,
    Show me I with Him have died.

No more let it be my working,
    Nor my wisdom, love, or power,
But the life of Jesus only,
    Passing through me hour by hour.

Let the fulness of Thy Spirit
    Resting on Him cover me,
That the witness borne to others,
    May bring glory, Lord, to Thee.

Father, in Thy Son's name pleading,
    I believe my prayer is heard;
And I praise Thee for the answer,
    Resting simply on Thy word.

    Praising now, praising now,
    Thou hast answered, Lord, I know!

              F. H. Allen.

Seven

Unusual Manifestations

"In the year that King Uzziah died I saw also the Lord sitting upon a throne, high and lifted up, and His train filled the temple . . . then said I 'Woe is me, for mine eyes have seen the king, the Lord of hosts" (Isa. 6:1-5).

"And I turned to see the voice that spake with me, and being turned, I saw seven golden candlesticks; and in the midst of the seven candlesticks one like unto the Son of Man . . . and when I saw Him, I fell at His feet as dead" (Rev. 1:12-17).

". . . I will love him, and will manifest myself to him" (John 14:21).

"Whatever emotions or high raptures may attend

such discoveries of the love and power of God in the case of some, they are not to be the tests and measures for all. Conversions are not alike in all, neither are the manifestations of the Spirit. He may come like the sun at high noon through rifted clouds, or like a slowly deepening dawn; like a shower or like the dew; like a great tide of air or like a gentle breeze; but all these worketh the one and self-same Spirit".   *Professor Erdman*

"EVERY STEP OF PROGRESS IN THE Christian life is taken by a fresh and a fuller appropriation of Christ by faith," says Charles Finney, "a fuller baptism of the Holy Spirit." The apostle Paul put it this way: "All of us with unveiled faces, reflecting like bright mirrors the glory of the Lord, are being transformed into the same likeness from one degree of radiant holiness to another, even as derived from the Lord the Spirit" (II Cor. 3:17-18 Weymouth). In the economy of grace, it is the ministry of the Lord, the Spirit, to conduct the believer into an ever-increasing knowledge of the glory of the Lord, that he might become conformed to the image of the Son of God (Romans 8:29). Oftentimes in performing this function of His ministry, the Spirit of holiness draws near to the believer in extraordinary manifestations, which Mr. Finney describes as "a fuller baptism of the Holy Spirit," but which many of us would refer to as "fresh anointings" or "fresh infillings." Whatever term we may use, one thing is certain: these experiences with God are real and enriching.

It may be said at the very outset that unusual manifestations are not always the experience of a child of God who enters into a fresh appropriation of Christ by faith. We are prone, both at conversion and at consecration, to come to the Lord with a preconceived idea of the exact sort of experience we are to have. Many times we demand the exact duplication of the experience of some famous saint of whom we have read, and are thus disappointed. We cannot dictate to Him the kind of feeling or emotion we so desire; we can only request reality in our experience. Reality is the thing that matters. We are not to be disturbed if we do not have the same intensity of feeling as do others, or if we have not experienced the same degree of exultation or supernatural manifestation which we hear others relate. The Spirit has His own way of revealing Christ to us and of leading us into deeper depths and greater heights of glory. And remember that the quiet dealing of the Spirit with Lydia, "whose heart the Lord opened," was just as definite and real as was that of the Philippian jailor who had an "earthquake experience." (Acts 16).

I verily believe, however, with Dr. A. J. Gordon, that if the Church of Jesus Christ was living today in vital, unbroken union with her beloved Head, we would see more frequently the power and glory of the Lord supernaturally manifested in our midst. It is a holy thrill to visit an assembly of believers in Wales, and to listen to the aged saints tell of the blessed scenes which took place during the Welsh Revival over fifty years ago. The moment there is opportunity, they will stand one by one, and with trembling voice and tear-stained face, relate the sacred incidents of those days just as if they had happened yesterday. The glory of those days has never left them.

Many times in the believer's pilgrim pathway, in the ordinary walk of obedience and faith, there comes high peaks in his spiritual experience when he receives such mighty manifestations of the presence of God that he is overwhelmed. It may be without warning that the Spirit comes upon the believer and fills his hungry soul with the love of Christ, so that he can only weep for joy. He repeats again and again in soul ecstasy with Paul, "The Son of God, Who loved me, and gave Himself for me!" At other times the Spirit moves in the heart of the child of God quietly but powerfully, and gives him an unutterable burden of intercession. At such times, the Paraclete Himself prays through the believer "with groanings which cannot be uttered." Occasionally a brother may be reading the Word with hungry heart, when the Spirit of Truth, in a unique manner, illuminates the sacred page, and gives such glorious views of the risen Lord, that he can only fall upon his knees in adoration and worship.

It may be when a group of believers have met definitely to seek the Lord's face that suddenly:

> Heaven comes down (their) souls to meet,
> And glory crowns the mercy seat.

Such was the experience of a group of God's servants who met together in Oxford, England, in the early days prior to the founding of the English Keswick Convention. These men, coming from different denominations, had come together to search the Scriptures and to look into their own hearts and lives to see whether there was not a wealth in Christ which they had not hitherto possessed. Many years later Canon Battersby, when presiding for his last time at the Keswick Convention in England, was led to tell of that occasion when he received a new revelation of Christ to his soul, "so extraordinary, glorious and precious, that from that day it has illuminated my life. I found that He was all I wanted. I shall never forget it; the day and the hour are present with me still. How it humbled me, yet what peace it brought!"

Some of us have had the experience of the disciples on the Emmaus road: "And it came to pass, as He sat at meat with them, He took bread, and blessed it, and brake, and gave to them, and their eyes were opened, and they knew Him; and He vanished out of their sight. And they said one to another, Did not our hearts burn within us while He talked with us by the way and while He opened to us the scriptures?" (Luke 24:30-32). I have known occasions during precious seasons of revival when believers were literally bathed in Calvary's Love by the precious Spirit, as He took of the treasures of Christ and revealed them to us. We have known an audience of several hundred souls to weep quietly for over an hour as the Spirit of Christ gave them a vision of their Lord in all His majesty, beauty and glory.

As we read the biographies of holy men and women of God down the years, we are startled to discover that most of them were favoured with unusual degrees of the revelation of the Lord. Such saints rapidly come to our minds: Martin Luther, Count Zinzendorf, Madame Guyon, Samuel Rutherford, Michael Peden, Jonathan Edwards, David Brainerd, James Brainerd Taylor, John Newton, William Cowper, Martin Boos, John Welsh, John Bunyan, Pastor Harms, Pastor Blumhardt, James Turner, George Muller, Dorothea Trudel, Sister Eva, Frank Crossley, William Pennefather, and a host of others. Surely what they experienced was nothing less than a fulfilment of the apostolic benediction: "Oh Father, let Thy love be manifested; Oh Lord Jesus, let Thy grace be with us; Oh Holy Spirit, let Thy saints enjoy much of Thy communion!"

We are often astonished to read of the experiences of

these Spirit-filled believers, because they are so extraordinary and far beyond anything that we have known in our own Christian life. We ask, "How can these things be?" We read, for example, of how Moody, Finney and others had to cry, "Oh God, stay Thy hand!" We hear of how Mr. Spurgeon got so lost "in the heavenlies" when in public prayer that he forgot the huge audience gathered to hear his sermon. It is not, however, a thing to be wondered at when one realizes that "we have this treasure in a fragile vase of clay" (II Cor. 4:7). How can the mortal body, which is the temple of the Holy Ghost, contain all the glory of the fulness of God! At the dedication of the Temple, the glory of the Lord so filled the house that the priests could not enter in; they could only prostrate themselves in worship (II Chron. 7:1-3). Ezekiel sat astonished seven days at the wonders of the dealings of God with his soul (Ezek. 3:15). Daniel swooned at the revelation of the Lord, when his strength completely left him. He cried out, "How can the servant of this my lord talk with this my lord?" (Daniel 10:17). Paul was caught up into the third heaven and could not tell whether he was in the body or out of the body (II Cor. 12:2-3). Who can read the writings of Samuel Rutherford, John Owen, Robert Hawker, or Nicholas of Basle, and not know that they were overwhelmed again and again with the majesty of God? Who can read the hymns of Tersteegen, Gerhardt, Cowper, Newton, Wesley, Watts, Hart, Bonar, Havergal and Crosby without recognizing their experiences of being overcome with the love of Christ?

We cannot close the meditations of these last three chapters concerning the extraordinary visitations of God to the soul, without warning the young believer concerning the pitfalls of Satan. There is, first of all, a danger that Satan will seek to give us a false experience

105

or a false revelation. We know of a man who has recorded so many visions he has received from the Lord
that he has become almost independent of the Word of
God! Edward Irving, a Presbyterian pastor in London,
was in his day held in highest esteem by his brethren
as one of the most spiritual and powerful evangelical
leaders. He lost his spiritual balance because he went
beyond the written Word of God. The temptations of
the Spirit-filled Christian are as great and as subtle as
were those of the Spirit-filled Christ in the wilderness.
Satan tempted our Lord to go beyond the written Word
of God, but was rebuked by our Lord when He said,
"It is written again, Thou shalt not tempt the Lord
Thy God" (Matt. 4:7).

Just as there are dangers of a counterfeit conversion,
a counterfeit consecration, and a counterfeit filling, so
there is a false or counterfeit revelation of the Spirit
given by Satan. In this matter, the Word of God is ever
our safeguard. The Spirit never speaks apart from or in
contradiction to the Word of God. Every revelation
and every manifestation must be tested in the light of
the doctrine of that inspired, unerring, infallible Book.
"Through Thy precepts I get understanding: therefore
I hate every false way. Thy Word is a lamp unto my feet
and a light unto my path" (Psalm 119:104,105). "To
the law and to the testimony; if they speak not according to this word, it is because there is no light in them"
(Isa. 8:20). "All Scripture is given by inspiration of
God, and is profitable for doctrine, for reproof, for cor-
rection, for instruction in righteousness: that the man
of God may be perfect, throughly furnished unto all
good works" (II Tim. 3:16,17).

There is also the danger of spiritual pride. Too often a
testimony given in meetings centers around the person
of the saint rather than the Person of the Saviour. It

diverts the attention of the hearers from the Lord to the recipient of His power. Colossians 1:18 is a verse we must never forget in our testimony meetings: "That in all things He might have the pre-eminence." "He must increase, but I must decrease" (John 3:30). Many who have known intimate relationship with the Lord have become backsliders because they have gloried in their experiences and become proud of themselves. Even Paul was in danger of glorying in his revelations, so that he was given a "thorn in the flesh," lest he should be exalted above measure. Mr. Moody only on rare occasions mentioned his first mighty experience with the Spirit of God on Wall Street, New York. We must walk prayerfully and carefully, lest we lose the anointing of the Spirit and the sweet manifestation of the Lord's presence. The deep, intimate, sacred dealings of God with the soul cannot be proclaimed from the housetops. It is only by direct permission from the Spirit Himself that we may be free to relate to others these experiences, and that for the glory of God alone.

We must ever be watchful lest self and Satan hinder the blessed Spirit in His endeavour to lead us into the light of the knowledge of the glory of God. Let us be ever ready, with prepared hearts, to receive by faith any fresh revelation of Christ which the Spirit would bring to our souls.

Come, Holy Ghost, our souls inspire,
And lighten with celestial fire.
Thou the anointing Spirit art,
Who dost Thy sevenfold gifts impart.
The blessed unction from above
In comfort, life, and fire of love.
Enable with perpetual light
The dullness of our blinded sight.
Anoint and cheer our soiled face
With the abundance of Thy grace.
Keep far our foes, give peace at home:
Where Thou art guide no ill can come.
Teach us to know the Father, Son,
And Thee of both to be but One,
That through the ages all along,
This may be our endless song:
Praise to Thy eternal merit,
Father, Son, and Holy Spirit!

(From Latin hymn of fourth century. Bishop John Cosin).

Eight

The Partnership of Pentecost

"True evangelism is working in cooperation with the Holy Spirit for the completion of the Body of Christ."   *J. A. S.*

"The Holy Spirit not only dwells in the Church as His habitation, but also uses her as a living organism whereby He moves and walks forth in the world, and speaks to the world, and acts upon the world. He is the Soul of the Church, which is Christ's Body."   *Bishop Webb*

"The Holy Spirit is omnipresent in the great Body of Christ; and omniscient in His oversight of the vast work of that Body in evangelizing the world."

A. T. Pierson

"The Gospel does not depend on any particular mode or fashion. If you have the Spirit, He will make His own methods. And it may be that God will have to dishonor agencies in which we have trusted if we are going to idolize them and so lose our trust in the Holy Ghost."

A. J. Gordon

ONE OF THE PRECIOUS TRUTHS CON-
cerning the ministry of the Spirit that has blessed my
own life has been that of partnership with His blessed
Person. Paul prayed fervently in his apostolic benediction, "The grace of the Lord Jesus Christ, and the love
of God, and the communion of the Holy Ghost be with
you all. Amen" (II Cor. 13:14). We are familiar
with the grace of the Lord Jesus, and with the love of
God, but what is our experience of the "communion of
the Holy Ghost?" The word translated "communion" is
the Greek word "koinonia," and is rendered "fellowship"
in Acts 2:42 and "partners" in Luke 5:10. What Paul
actually invoked for the Corinthian saints was, "The
fellowship or *partnership* of the Holy Ghost be with
you all." This experience of partnership with the Spirit
in the supreme work of evangelism was predicted by
our Lord in the Upper Room when He said, "But when
the Comforter is come, whom I will send unto you from
the Father, even the Spirit of truth, which proceedeth
from the Father, He shall testify of me: And ye also
shall bear witness" (John 15:26-27).

In the four Gospels, we find that up to this time, the

Holy Spirit had exclusively occupied the Person of the Son of God. Christ lived His entire life from Bethlehem to the Ascension in the power of the Spirit. But now the disciples were told that the same blessed Spirit, Who energized and controlled the life of their Lord, was to energize and control their lives. At Pentecost they would enter into a new partnership with this august Person. Then they would understand the startling statement: "Verily, verily, I say unto you, he that believeth in me, the works that I do shall he do also; and greater works than these shall he do; because I go unto my Father" (John 14:12).

There was a young man named Archibald Brown who had a flaming heart to preach the Evangel. He was received by Mr. Spurgeon into the Pastors' College. Later he began a highly successful ministry as pastor of the East London Tabernacle. One has often wondered how this young man must have felt as a contemporary of C. H. Spurgeon, when he began his work as a pastor and evangelist. Surely many times in the secret place before God he bemoaned his lack of the mighty gifts which were so plainly evident in his friend and elder brother. Yet as time went on, his own tabernacle was filled with thousands of people, as he ministered to them under the mighty anointing of the Spirit. He saw apostolic blessing year after year in his own ministry; so much so that I believe Archibald Brown (apart from the Olney brothers, Spurgeon's senior deacons) was more intimate in spiritual fellowship with Mr. Spurgeon than any other man. Here with this dear brother, Spurgeon could have real intimate heart communion in the deep things of God. The secret of his power and spirituality was discovered in his well thumbed Bible after his death. There is a little note in the margin beside the twenty-eighth verse of the fifteenth chapter of the Acts: "The senior partnership of the Holy Ghost! Neither Christian life nor Christian service are worth anything apart from this partnership." It may be said that the measure we enjoy of the fellowship with our Senior Partner is the measure of blessing in our life and witness.

In the Acts of the Apostles, the Church's text-book of evangelism and church life, we see recorded in every chapter, and in almost every incident, this fellowship and partnership with the Holy Spirit. The two key verses of the Book are Acts 9:31 and 1:8. The secret of all blessing was the fact that they "walked in the comfort (or paraklesis) of the Holy Ghost." The verse literally says that they walked in the "paraklesis" of the "Paraclete"; in other words, they lived their entire lives in moment by moment fellowship with the "One-called-alongside-to-help"! By such a walk they experienced such a ministry as promised in chapter one, verse eight: "But ye shall receive power, after that the Holy Ghost is come upon you: and ye shall be witnesses unto me, both in Jerusalem, and in all Judaea, and in Samaria, and unto the uttermost part of the earth." Also in this verse we see that true evangelism is working in co-operation with the Holy Spirit for the completion of the body of Christ.

The disciples were commanded not to depart from Jerusalem to begin their work in their own zeal, but to wait for the promise of the Father. They must not lift a tiny finger nor take a single step. How strange and difficult this must have been to a temperament and personality like Peter's! One can visualize Peter restlessly pacing up and down the room, and probably walking impatiently through the narrow streets of Jerusalem. "Why wait, when the world is perishing? We have our orders; why don't we begin our crusade?" They must

113

wait, because they could not begin their ministry without the Senior Partner. Their ministry would have been entirely in vain apart from this fellowship. The Holy Ghost was to be given, to empower the disciples supernaturally to take the Gospel to every creature.

In the fifth chapter of Acts, we have the second persecution of the Church, when the apostles stand before the council and witness to the verities of our Lord's death, resurrection and ascension, and to the sinner's responsibility towards this doctrine. Even though they have been imprisoned, they are fearless, because they are conscious that the Holy Spirit is with them to confirm their witness with power. They cry, "The God of our fathers raised up Jesus, whom ye slew and hanged on a tree. Him hath God exalted with his right hand to be a Prince and a Saviour, for to give repentance to Israel, and forgiveness of sins. And we are His witnesses of these things; and so is also the Holy Ghost" (vv. 30-32). Note that in the very same verse the apostles say that they are witnesses to this doctrine and so is also the Holy Ghost. In commenting on this verse, Campbell Morgan says, "That is the Church's final power. That is the mightiest fact of all. If we lack co-ordination with the Holy Spirit; unless we are in business partnership with the Holy Spirit, we can do nothing to impress Jerusalem or London. Unless the preacher is touched with the Unseen, unless the Church catches and flashes upon the world the mystic light of the infinite, which cannot be gathered in the academy or university, preacher and church will be 'faultily faultless, icily regular, splendidly null'. If we would fill London with our doctrine, we must be in partnership with the Holy Spirit. Then, through joy and pain, the Church will move forward with God in continual victory."

114

We see next two individual believers working in partnership with the Spirit. In the eighth chapter we find Philip in the midst of a blessed time of revival in the city of Samaria. How glorious to see a deacon conducting evangelistic meetings! Oh that the Church today would go "everywhere, preaching the Word!" From these scenes of triumph an angel of the Lord commanded Philip to go down to the desert. How extraordinary! Surely, man's ways are not God's ways. If there had been an evangelistic committee taking care of Philip's campaign in that city, they would have strongly objected, and said to Philip, "Dear brother, you must be mistaken. God would not ask you to do such a thing. He is mightily blessing you here. You have not truly heard the voice of the Spirit." Philip also could have reasoned thus: "Blessed Spirit, could you not find some 'desert evangelist' to carry out this ministry for you? You see I am very busy, and besides, I am a city preacher. My brethren would not understand my leaving them and going to a desert to preach. There is also a possibility that if the people hear that I go to deserts to preach to small crowds, they may not come out in great numbers to hear me again. I would lose my prestige. They would say I was eccentric if I told them I was going down to the desert, just because You told me to do so. Oh Lord, Thou knowest how many practical-minded believers there are here!"

The thing that strikes me most in this incident is that Philip did not know for what purpose was the Spirit's call. Like Abraham, he went out not knowing what would be the ultimate result of his journey. It was only when he reached the desert that he found the work the Lord had for him. What a tremendous step of faith this was! He obeyed the Lord because he knew he was working in partnership with the Spirit; it was not for him to decide alone the time and sphere of his labours. Dear Christian worker, it is a great tower of strength to know that the Spirit of Pentecost has a divine strategy for worldwide evangelism. I believe that Philip, by winning this one soul in the desert, had a more far-reaching ministry than if he had continued in Samaria. We must never despise the day of small things.

In one of the Presbyterian churches in Scotland the people asked for the resignation of their pastor, because they could see very little results from his ministry. "But what about Robert?" he asked. "Oh," they said, "he is only a child of twelve years." The old preacher replied, "But he has a life before him." The boy was Robert Moffatt, the mighty missionary who pioneered in Africa with the Gospel, and was the means of the salvation of thousands. His daughter married another Scottish missionary, David Livingstone, and thus the fruitfulness of the labours of the old pastor was continued.

If Philip had been a modern evangelist, he possibly would have taken out his diary, and said, "Oh Lord of the Harvest, I am sorry I cannot go now, because you see here how I am solidly booked ahead for the next two years! Another time you can invite me, when I have an open date." While conversing with evangelical leaders over the past thirty years in different continents, I have found that the consensus of opinion is that it is ridiculous to try to follow apostolic principles in a modern age. Thus, the supernatural guidance of the Holy Spirit in evangelistic work both at home and on the mission field is sometimes scorned. I believe that the real reason for this attitude is that our Church and evangelistic machinery is so expensive and cumbersome, and so highly organized, that there is no room left for the free, spontaneous, supernatural work of the Spirit. I say kindly that I do not believe any precious man or woman of God can stand up and declare publicly that he knows definitely he has been called by the Holy Ghost to every one of these places mentioned in his diary for the next two or three years. Furthermore, I do not believe that he knows of a truth in his heart, that the Spirit wants him to stay in one town or village for one or two days, and to stay in another place for a month. I am all for decency and order in the arrangement of our Christian work, but I am sure that many times the Holy Spirit is grieved exceedingly because we do not ask His guidance, not only concerning the sphere, but also the length of time He has planned for us to stay in a place.

Stephen Grellet, the Quaker business man, was suddenly commanded by the Spirit to leave New York City and go and preach to the lumber-men in the lumber camps in the backwoods of Canada. On his arrival, he discovered to his dismay that the lumber-men had moved further north and had left empty camps. Having walked with God and obeyed the Spirit constantly for years, it was no test of faith for Stephen Grellet to stand in an empty canteen hall in an empty camp and preach to nobody! It was not until many years later, however, that he understood the meaning of his mission. One day in the street in New York City he was accosted by a stranger, who told him that he was the man whom God had used to be the means of his conversion. He related the following story: One day he had been sent back by his foreman for some tool left behind in the lumber camp, and on approaching the camp he was startled to hear, as it were, a voice from heaven. He knew that the camp was empty. Following the direction of the voice, he was amazed to discover a solitary figure standing on a platform, preaching to nobody! He was so frightened at this strange sight that he left the camp

117

as quickly as possible. However, the words from the Holy Scriptures which fell from Stephen Grellet's lips found a lodging-place in his heart and conscience, and were the means of his regeneration.

The evangelical world has been thrilled at the mighty workings of the Holy Spirit in the Hebrides of Scotland. On one occasion Mr. Duncan Campbell was ministering at a Convention in Northern Ireland, and was about to go to the building to deliver his conference address, when suddenly the Spirit told him to go at once to one of the islands in the Hebrides. The chairman, being a spiritual man, and knowing something of the supernatural work of God, readily consented that our brother should go immediately. On arriving at the lonely island, the evangelist found that the saints were awaiting him to begin his preaching ministry. They had not sent him a letter of invitation, and yet the Holy Spirit had revealed to them that he was coming and that they should prepare the meetings. Needless to say, they gathered under an "open heaven."

In my own ministry, I could repeat story after story of this same blessed compulsion of the Spirit. While labouring in the Orkney Islands, as a young man, suddenly the Spirit spoke to me, bidding me leave my fruitful evangelistic ministry in Great Britian and go to the city of Riga in far off Latvia. One can imagine the surprised look on the faces of the congregation when, in that Presbyterian Church that night, I announced that the campaign was over, and I was going now to begin to evangelize the Russians. On my arrival home to Glasgow, it was very hard for my loved ones to believe that the Spirit had called me thus. When other believers in Britain heard that I had started out on such a "wild venture," they were sure I was fanatical. "God may work in such a manner with the apostles in the early

118

days, but not with His servants in these modern days,"
they said. Their reasonings were logical in the natural.
Everything was contrary to the way man would guide
and work. Yet, upon that obedience to the supernatural
call, humanly speaking, depended the salvation of thousands of souls, as well as the founding of a Missionary
Society which has over one hundred missionaries today.

See the split-second guidance of the Lord of the Harvest in the case of Philip! It is not easy to find a man in
a desert! At the exact moment he arrived, he found a
man of Ethiopia sitting in a chariot reading a scroll of
Isaiah. This dear man had gone to Jerusalem to find
God, but had received stones for bread. He could not
find the Saviour in all the ritualism. His heart was heavy.
He was now going back home to die in the darkness of
heathenism. If he found no help at Jerusalem, however,
he at least brought back with him a scroll of the sacred
writings. Would you say it was "by chance" or a coin-
cidence that he was reading the fifty-third chapter when
the Holy Ghost said to Philip, "Go near and join thyself
to this chariot"? What better chapter could one use to
preach the unsearchable riches of Christ! "He was
wounded for our transgressions and bruised for our ini-
quities." Upon the diplomat's confession of faith in Jesus
Christ as Lord, the "Spirit of the Lord caught away
Philip, that the eunuch saw him no more; and he went
on his way rejoicing." The man went away rejoicing and
Philip went away preaching. The deacon-evangelist's
work was completed and the Spirit of the Lord carried
him away to another field of witness.

In the tenth chapter we find the other individual,
Peter, also working under the partnership of the Spirit.
Here once again we are shown the value that God
places upon the salvation of one single soul. We must
never forget that the greatest Gospel text of all—John

3:16—was spoken to one man at the midnight hour. Sometimes, even on the mission field, personal soul winning has far deeper results than preaching to large crowds. You may win one person for Christ, who, in turn, will win large numbers. It is the partnership of the Spirit that counts!

The Spirit needs now another worker to carry the Gospel to a captain of the Italian regiment named Cornelius, who was quartered at Caesarea. He was deeply religious, but not saved. He was crying to God for the light of the Gospel. The Spirit had worked already on the heart of the Gentile and prepared him for the reception of the evangel. Now the Spirit had to prepare His instrument who was to bring the glad tidings. Peter was a bigoted believer, who did not want to have fellowship even with Gentile believers, much less the heathen! The Lord was preparing him for a wider ministry, and so we find in verse six that he was lodging "with one Simon a tanner." The trade of a tanner was held in such contempt by the Jews that in many cities he had to build his house fifty cubits outside the city. Staying with Simon the tanner down by the seaside, was preparing Peter for this wider ministry among the Gentiles. It was while Peter was on the housetop praying that he received a vision, followed by a revelation from the Spirit. "While Peter thought on the vision, the Spirit said unto him, Behold, three men seek thee." This amazing chapter of the Acts has been repeated again and again on the Mission Field —a prepared heart meeting with a prepared servant.

Peter, against all his natural prejudices, obeyed the voice of the Spirit and accompanied the men to the house of Cornelius. What a receptive audience! In our prayers we must ask always for prepared hearts for the reception of the seed we are about to sow. After expounding the way of salvation, God's servant closed with these blessed words, "To Him give all the prophets witness that through His Name, whosoever believeth in Him shall receive remission of sins." While Peter was speaking these words, suddenly the Spirit fell on all the hearers. Oh dear Christian worker, if you will go forth and talk under the guidance of the Spirit, He will corroborate everything you say. The Jewish law required that there should be two witnesses in a testimony. Here we find the Holy Spirit as the second witness. Whether preaching to crowds or talking to a solitary individual, we must keep crying to the Holy Spirit to confirm the Word.

What a rich blessing Peter would have missed had he delayed obedience to the voice of the Spirit! I know an aged Russian evangelist who, in God's hands, has been instrumental in the salvation of thousands of souls, but who missed one glorious opportunity to witness, because he did not obey the Spirit's injunction to go and speak to the famous Russian author, Tolstoi. Tolstoi did not attend the Gospel meetings of our brother, but his wife did, and recorded it in her diary as a very important event. It was discovered after the author's death that for the last few months of his life he had travelled from one monastery to another in Russia, seeking the way of salvation. The Spirit had spoken to my friend about visiting the author and speaking to him concerning the claims of Christ, but during the crowded days he had delayed the visit. When finally he arrived at the home of Mr. Tolstoi he found him too ill to see him. The opportunity had passed.

In the thirteenth chapter we no longer have an individual, but a local assembly of the Lord's people in partnership with the Spirit. We read that "as they ministered to the Lord, and fasted, the Holy Ghost said, "Separate me Barnabas and Saul for the work whereunto

121

I have called them." Let us notice the circumstances under which the Spirit of God spoke to them. They were ministering to the Lord. Now it does not say they were ministering the Gospel to the unsaved here, or ministering food and clothing to the poor; they were ministering TO THE LORD. This ministry is a lost art. That is the reason why we have so few New Testament churches today. We are too busy in the work to be busy in the admiration of our Lord. Our ministry will be cold and lifeless unless we have a deep appreciation of the Person of the Lord Jesus. Ministering to the Lord is worshipping God. True worship is heart occupation with the Son of God. It is the assembly's joy and glory in the Lamb of God that delights the Father's heart. Worship is more important than service, because all true service springs from worship. How sad that we are too busy today to minister to the Lord! Even our Communion Services for "the breaking of bread" are hurried over, that the people might rush home for dinner. What a blessing would come to our churches if we could have a longer time to worship the Lord unhurriedly in the beauty of holiness.

> Gracious God, we worship Thee,
>   Rev'rently we bow the knee;
> Jesus Christ, our only plea:
>   Father, we adore Thee.

> Vast Thy love, how deep, how wide,
>   In the gift of Him Who died;
> Righteous claims all satisfied;
>   Father, we adore Thee.

> Lo, we bow before Thy face,
>   Sons of God, oh wondrous place;
> Great the riches of Thy grace:
>   Father, we adore Thee.

By Thy Spirit grant that we
   Worshippers in truth may be;
Praise, as incense sweet to Thee:
   Father, we adore Thee.

Yet again our song we raise,
   Note of deep adoring praise;
Now, and soon through endless days:
   Father, we adore Thee.

Trevor Francis.

Now in a song of grateful praise,
   To Thee, O Lord, my voice I'll raise;
With all Thy saints I'll join to tell
   My Saviour has done all things well!

We are also told that *they fasted*. During the fasting time they were interceding on behalf of the Church and the world. All the hosts of hell were arrayed against them, and they were crying for a fresh outpouring of the Holy Spirit in their midst. Once again, we see how far we have wandered from the apostolic pattern. How few churches ever have days of fasting and prayer to cry to God for mighty blessing! Spurgeon cried, "We must honour the Spirit; unless we put Him first He will never make crowns for us to wear. He will get victories, but He will have the honour of them; and if we do not give Him the honour, He will never give us the privilege and success. And, best of all, if you would have the Holy Spirit, let us meet together earnestly to pray for Him. Remember, the Holy Spirit will not come to us as a Church unless we seek Him. 'For this thing will I be inquired of all the House of Israel to do it for them.' We purpose during the coming week to hold meetings of special prayer to supplicate for Revival .... Let us meet and pray, and if God doth not hear us it will be the first time He has broken His promise."

Fasting and prayer go together. Many churches cannot find time for prayer because they are too occupied with other things. When a Church fasts sincerely, her members are placed in a spiritual frame of mind and heart which enables them to prevail mightily in prayer. As they fast and pray, they find the anointing of the Spirit upon them, and they are "inside the vail," touching the Throne. The Moravians fasted. The Hussites fasted. The Waldensians fasted. The Huguenots fasted. The Scottish Covenanters fasted. And they all prayed down blessing from heaven. When was the last time the Holy Spirit spoke to your assembly? Have you, as a group, been quiet enough before Him to hear His voice? It is a very solemn contemplation that the Spirit might have wanted to talk with your assembly, but could not make Himself heard. Surely this thought must cause us all to tremble. What a tragedy to have missed the mind of the Spirit for the assembly, even as for our own private lives! At the judgment seat of Christ will it be revealed to you and me that the Spirit of God had many things to reveal to us but could not because we were not in a condition to hear? How necessary it is for us to learn the lesson of holy quietness before the Lord at the throne of grace.

When the Spirit speaks there is no confusion. In the above instance, He not only revealed His will to the assembly, but also to Saul and Barnabas. The Spirit told both parties His plan. If He calls anyone from your midst, He will surely make it plain also to others in the assembly who are walking in partnership with Him. We believe that if a brother is called by the Spirit from an assembly for full-time Christian work, He will have a good testimony and a good commendation from his brethren. On the other hand, there is no use laying hands upon a brother or sister, if the Holy Ghost has not laid hands on them. The Spirit's call is the first and fundamental factor that enters into all Christian service. This is one of the provinces of the Spirit into which man dare not intrude or interfere.

Notice how emphatic are the words of the Spirit: Separate me—set apart to me—these brethren "WHOM I HAVE CALLED." We detect in this statement the authority of the Lord of the Harvest. Only the Spirit can call. And when the Spirit calls, it is UNTO HIMSELF, and not unto an assembly or society. "Separate them unto Me, for I have a distinctive work for them to do." The worker is first of all a separated servant unto the Lord, and he is responsible to the Spirit alone. He has been called and set apart by the Spirit, unto the Spirit, as His messenger for a special set-apart work, which he alone can accomplish, and that by the Spirit's power alone.

It is well to pause here for a moment, however, to consider the fact of labouring together as a group or society, such as a church, or evangelistic agency, or missionary society. For example, in the case of a missionary society, there is a director and an executive board at the home base, and on the field, usually a field director and executive field committee comprised of senior missionaries of that society, who seek to oversee and direct the work. If a brother or sister feels led of the Lord to work in fellowship with any society on the mission field, he certainly will seek to work in harmony with those directing the work. He must never forget that they also have the indwelling Holy Spirit, and, if filled with the Spirit, are also seeking His divine guidance for the affairs of the whole field. A missionary must be careful to recognize and appreciate the leading of the Holy Spirit in his brothers and sisters. We know that the human element will often enter in, as it did with Barnabas and Saul early in their ministry together, when there

was a sharp contention over John Mark (Acts 15:36-40).
The word "contention" is rendered "to provoke" in
Hebrews 10:24, and is the Greek word from which we
derive our English word "paroxysm," meaning "a sudden
violent action or emotion." It was a serious disagreement
between two leading brothers who had been set apart
by the Spirit and unto the Spirit. But the Spirit over-
ruled, so that as far as we know, the work was not hin-
dered. When Mark had been with Barnabas for some
time he was later restored to Paul's fellowship, for when
Paul wrote to the Colossian Church he spoke of Mark
as his fellow-worker and commended him to the saints
in Colossae (Col. 4:10). The harmony of the Spirit may
be maintained through individual humble submission
to Him in all things. It must be emphasized that in the
last analysis the worker is responsible to the Holy Spirit
for his ministry: "Separate me Barnabas and Saul for
the work whereunto I have called them."

In verses three and four we seem to find a contradiction. In verse three we read that after the Church
had laid hands on them "they sent them away." In verse
four we read that they were "sent forth by the Holy
Ghost." The truth is that the Church at Antioch was so
one with the Spirit, that when they sent them away, we
are told that the Holy Ghost sent them away. Oh blessed
partnership! *Oh how glorious it would be if every delib-
eration and decision of our boards and committees could
be said to be that of the Holy Ghost!* How much arguing
and sharp contention could be avoided in these executive meetings, if only the mind of the Spirit were sought
beforehand in the secret place, and then together, in
quietness and submission, before the Lord of the Harvest.

Let us go now to the fifteenth chapter. Here is not the
individual assembly, but the first general council of all

the churches. There was a warm theological controversy which was about to wreck the young Church upon the rock of doctrinal dispute. James summed up his presidential address with these arresting words: "It seemed good to the Holy Ghost, and to us" (v. 28). How few chairmen at any evangelical gathering would have the courage today to utter these words? They seem strange and somewhat fanatical to many evangelical ears, so far have we drifted from apostolic standards. Some of us would have said, "It seemed to doctor so and so, and it seems good to me." And then, in order to be evangelical and fundamental, we might say, "Oh yes, and it seemed good to the Holy Ghost." James gave the Holy Spirit the first place, and so must it ever be, if we are going to have the smile of God upon our labours. Nothing but confusion can come to any church or organization that gives the Holy Spirit a lesser place in our midst than that of Senior Partner. The modern churches invite the Holy Spirit to come in after all the business has been conducted. Some helpful brother suggests that it would be good if we could have a prayer meeting to ask the Holy Spirit to bless the decisions already agreed upon!

We want revival, but are we prepared to ask the Holy Spirit to come and be the Chairman of our gatherings? Are we prepared to stand aside and allow the Spirit of God to exalt the Lord Jesus in our midst? How many times the Spirit is grieved and quenched, because some wealthy sister or some worldly business man runs the affairs of the church. When the Spirit of God takes full control, there will be drastic changes in the affairs of the assembly. It will cost and it will hurt. Are you willing to unitedly cry now, "Oh, Spirit of Pentecost, take first place"?

We close our study with the sixteenth chapter. Here

127

is the great crisis chapter; a crisis in the history of global evangelism. The divine record reads, "Now when they had gone throughout Phrygia and the region of Galatia, and were forbidden of the Holy Ghost to preach the Word in Asia, after they were come to Mysia, they assayed to go into Bithynia: but the Spirit suffered them not" (vv. 6, 7). In this incident we see the restraining hand of the Spirit upon the apostles. They were "forbidden of the Holy Ghost to preach the Word in Asia"! They attempted to go into Bithynia, "but the Spirit suffered them not." As the thirteenth chapter reveals to us that a man must be called by the Spirit to service, so chapter sixteen emphasizes the fact that the Spirit must direct us into our fields of labour. Basically, every born-again Christian worker believes that the Holy Spirit must control his movements, and yet how often we allow human circumstances to dictate the decision. How many pastors and evangelists allow money, prestige, housing facilities, educational advantages, and the like, to influence their leaving or remaining in a field of labour. We believe that if we obey the voice of the Spirit, He will take care of all other needs.

The Lord of the Harvest guides in different ways. We must not criticise each other. Paul did not force these two doors, once the Spirit had closed them. He knew he was working in partnership with the Spirit, and no blessing could accrue if he disobeyed His guidance. Sometimes God has a riper and richer field for His servant. Sometimes, unexpectedly, a new door opens of which he had not conceived. H. Grattan Guinness, while a mighty world-famous evangelist and Bible teacher, late in life was called to begin "The Regions Beyond Missionary Union." The Holy Spirit is working to a divine strategy for worldwide evangelism, and He places His men and women where He chooses. Sometimes He takes a John Hunter and sends him into Turk-estan to labour alone in pioneer mission work; or He takes a William C. Burns from mighty revival work in Scotland and sends him to heathen China. Another time He takes a Catherine Booth-Clibborn and sends her into the "lion's mouth" of a wicked city like Paris. The one specific lesson we must all learn is that the Spirit is the absolute Lord of the Harvest, and we must look to Him for guidance and direction. The Spirit will not always guide us into fruitful fields of labour. He may lead us to do the hard work of ploughing and sowing. He may lead us to labour for years among the Moslems before the harvest is reaped. The Spirit will not always lead us into paths of easy service, but we must be prepared to follow His guidance at all cost. Paul, the glorious pastor, mis-sionary, evangelist and Bible teacher, cries "And now, behold I go bound in the Spirit unto Jerusalem, not knowing the things that shall befall me there: save that the Holy Ghost witnesseth in every city, saying that bonds and afflictions abide me" (Acts 20:22-23). The apostle to the Gentiles knew that imprisonment and possibly death lay ahead of him, but he triumphantly declared, "None of these things move me."

> None of these things move me,
>   If Christ in the conflict be
> The world may assail and demons may rail;
>   But none of these things move me.

Why was Paul unmoved? Simply because he was being led "bound in the Spirit." He knew that the Spirit was guiding him according to His great plan and purpose.

Dr. A. J. Gordon remarks, "Very striking is this record of the ever-present, unfailing and minute direction of the Holy Ghost in all the steps of this divine enterprise.

'But this was in apostolic days,' it will be said. Yes; but the promise of the Spirit is that 'He shall abide with you for the age.' Unless the age has ended He is still there and still in office, and still entrusted with the responsibility of carrying out that work which is dearest to the heart of our glorified Lord. Who can say that there is not need in these days of a return to primitive methods and of a resumption of the Church's primitive endowments? The Holy Spirit is not straitened in Himself, but only in us. If the Church had faith to lean less on human wisdom, to trust less in prudential methods, to administer less by mechanical rules, and to recognize once more the great fact that, having committed to her a supernatural work, she has appointed for her a supernatural power, who can doubt that the grinding and groaning of our cumbrous missionary machinery would be vastly lessened and the demonstration of the Spirit be far more apparent?" Oh that the grace of the Lord Jesus Christ, the love of God, and the partnership of the Holy Ghost may be with you all! Amen.

Nine

Leakage of Divine Power

"I once heard a Scot preacher say that Satan does not act as if he believes in the final persevorence of the saints. He comes back again; he knows the way; he has the latch-key in his pocket; he knows the avenues of entrance; he comes seeking admission, and if he finds within our citadel a place for him he always takes possession of the unoccupied spaces. He may return transformed as an angel of light, but an unclean spirit still. Is there no danger of such things? I believe there is; I believe there was never more danger than there is in the days in which we live. 'Let him that thinketh he standeth take heed lest he fall.' What is the preventive of a danger so alarming? I only know of one—it is to be

131

God-possessed. It is to let the flag of Calvary float from the floor to the roof, and from the turret to the dungeon of the castle of your being; it is to let God be in possession. Light expels darkness; health expels disease; God turns out Satan."

E. W. Moore

W E APPROACH OUR THEME WITH UNSAN-
dalled feet, walking softly before our God. ". . . let us
have grace, whereby we may serve God acceptably with
reverence and godly fear: For our God is a consuming
fire" (Hebrews 12:28-29). Surely there is no more
solemn subject in the entire life of the believer than that
of the leakage of spiritual power.

SAMSON

Samson is set forth in the Word of God as a beacon
light: a warning to all Christian workers. Called and
commissioned for a specific ministry, Samson was a
mighty instrument of blessing. He was an enigma to the
lords of the Philistines. His very name struck terror in
the hearts of the enemy. Yet this deliverer lost his
spiritual power.

Samson's defeat began with an unholy alliance. Samson played with sin. No man or woman can take fire into
the bosom, and not be burned. "Can a man take fire in
his bosom, and his clothes not be burned?" (Proverbs
6:27). The vampire bat will fan its victim to sleep while

it sucks his blood. Sin does its deadly work, although the soul may be unconscious of its ravages.

Samson played with his holy consecrated vows (Numbers 6:1). He lost the holy awe of the Spirit's unction. Notice his boasting: "Bind me with cords and then I shall have no strength: . . . . bind me with ropes and I shall not have strength" (Judges 16:7,11). When Samson began to regard as a light thing his sacred annointing, he soon began to descend to lying. Samson could rend lions and conquer the Philistines, but he could not conquer his appetites. It is said that paralysis comes upon its victim unconsciously. So with the loss of spiritual power. "And he wist not that the Lord was departed from him." There is a sense in which we are the first ones to know of any secret declension, yet there is another sense in which oftentimes spiritual people can discern that we have lost the anointing. See what poor Samson lost—his power, his vision, his liberty; and alas, he became the plaything of the world. Is there anything more tragic in the Scriptures than the mighty giant's name becoming a by-word of mockery among the Philistines! What a solemn reminder for us, that he was buried at the same place in which the Spirit of God began to move him in the beginning (Judges 13:25; 16:31).

Because he did not know of his spiritual loss, Samson began to go out as at any other time in the power of the Spirit, but suddenly discovered he was "like any other man." It is also possible for us to be active Christian workers, and be unconscious of our spiritual loss. However, like with Samson, in the time of crisis, our spiritual condition will surely manifest itself. Samson, in the presumption of the flesh, thought he needed only to shake himself as before, and the power of God would automatically be upon him. Increased activity in the service of God will not recover this unction.

Every one of us knows that there is a tremendous possibility, after having received the Baptism, or after several subsequent anointings, of losing this supernatural power. English atomic scientists have used their knowledge to detect leaks in water pipes. Knowing that some of the joints in the pipe-line were leaking, they injected radio-active sodium into the cistern and then walked over the ground with geiger counters. At the two points in the line where the leaks existed, the geiger counters picked up the radio-active water, and the leaking joints were quickly repaired. In like manner, if we will allow the Holy Spirit to search our hearts and lives, He will quickly point out the places where there is spiritual leakage.

May I suggest a number of ways whereby we can lose the mighty anointing.

CRITICISM

Criticism is necessary. We need constructive criticism from keenly spiritual persons. It is good for us to get together in private conferences or retreats for constructive criticisms concerning the work of the Lord, but we must always search our hearts and see what is the motive behind our criticism. Some Christians seem to think it is their definite ministry, received from our ascended Lord, to criticise everything and everybody. Unless our criticism springs from Calvary's love, it is utterly sinful. Hear the wise words of Richard Baxter to the jealous ministers of his day, "What! malign Christ in gifts for which He should have the glory, and all because they seem to hinder our glory! Does not every man owe thanks to God for his brethren's gifts—not only as having himself part in them, as the foot has the benefit of the guidance of the eye, but also because his own ends may be attained by his brethren's gifts as well as by his own? .... A fearful thing that any man that hath the least of the fear of God, should so envy at God's gifts, that he would rather his carnal hearers were unconverted, and the drowsy not awakened, than that it should be done by another who may be preferred before him."

GOSSIP

Samson lost his power because he talked too much. Samson lost his power when he told all he knew. The talkative Christian is usually a powerless Christian. We need to pray, like the Psalmist, "Set a watch, O Lord, before my mouth; keep the door of my lips" (Psalm 141:3). There is a tremendous dissipation of power when our speech is not seasoned with salt. (Col. 4:6)

How often, after a most blessed time in the prayer meeting, we have lost the blessing through idle talk and gossip.

AN UNFORGIVING SPIRIT

Another cause of the leakage of divine power is allowing a root of bitterness to spring up in our hearts because of a wrong inflicted upon us. An unforgiving spirit will blight spiritual fruit, and also cause a deep shadow to come between you and your Lord. We must remember that at all times it is the reaction to the incident or source of conflict that matters more than the incident itself. The incident will soon pass away, but the effect upon our spiritual life does not. The most important question is not whether we are right or wrong, but whether we have been kept from resentment and have an inward sweetness. Do we genuinely love those who have wronged us?

136

Hudson Taylor, commenting on the blessed adversity of Job, wrote as follows: "Even Satan did not presume to ask God to be allowed himself to afflict Job. In the first chapter and the eleventh verse he says: 'Put forth Thine hand and touch his bone and his flesh, and he will curse Thee to Thy face.' Satan knew that none but God could touch Job; and when Satan was permitted to afflict him, Job was quite right in recognizing the Lord Himself as the Doer of these things which He permitted to be done. Oft-times we should be helped and blessed if we would bear in mind that Satan is servant and not master, and that he and wicked men incited are only permitted to do that which God by His determinate counsel and foreknowledge has before determined shall be done. Come joy or come sorrow, we may always take it from the hand of God."

How the tendency to wrong feeling and resentment would be removed, could we take an injury from the hand of a loving Father, instead of looking chiefly at the agent through which it comes! It matters not who is the messenger—it is with God that His children have to do. Yes, we must refuse to look at second causes.

Do you 'neath injustice smart?
Do wrongs rankle in your heart?
Ponder this, and cease to fret,
　　"I forgave thee all that debt!"

If your injuries should rise
Till they reach the very skies—
O'er them all could this be said
　　"I forgave thee all that debt!"

Your great liability
Nailed your Saviour to the tree.
Knowing this, do you forget
　　He forgave you all that debt?

Can it be you still forbear
Swift forgiveness to declare
Your fellow-servant—Yet
You were pardoned all that debt!

"I forgave thee"—Blessed Lord,
Write upon my heart this word!
Cause me never to forget
    "I forgave thee all that debt!"

Paul exhorts us: "And be ye kind one to another, tender-hearted, forgiving one another, even as God for Christ's sake has forgiven you." "Be ye therefore followers of God, as dear children; and walk in love, as Christ also hath loved us" (Ephes. 4:32; 5:1).

FRIVOLITY

While it is true that Christ "hath been anointed with the oil of gladness above His fellows" (Heb. 1:9), and that the "fruit of the Spirit is . . . . joy" (Gal. 5:22), and that "the joy of the Lord is your strength" (Neh. 8:10), nevertheless, the Christian life is not one of carnal frivolity. There is a vast difference between the "pepped-up" meetings where natural soulish joy is demonstrated, and a meeting where the joy of the Lord floods and fills the believers. What a difference between the spiritual "glory-hallelujah" shoutings of Bible saints, and the cheap, jazzy, soul-destroying ones of modern-day Christians. The former was the overflow of souls flooded with the glory and power of God, while the latter is nothing but the hilarious expression of the flesh trying to "have a good time" and work up some carnal emotions. Let us never forget that we are dealing with weighty eternal matters; matters that affect lives for time and eternity. Let us remember that we must give an account at the "Bema" for our flippancy in Christian service. How we have winced and groaned in spirit at the vulgar, cheap lightness manifested by so-called young evangelical believers. The Christian life is not a sporting event, circus, or fun-fair.

HUMOUR

Humour is a gift of God. It is very blessed and refreshing when there is a brother or sister with a keen sense of humour on the mission field, one who can appreciate a joke on himself as well as on others. God has always used sanctified humour. Scottish John McNeil, the evangelist so highly used by God with Mr. Moody, had a tremendous sense of humour, and a capacity for wit. God used this trait in a marvellous way to the salvation of precious souls. Nevertheless, humour in the pulpit is a dangerous thing. You are handling dynamite. Very few can sanctify humour at the sacred desk. How often we have seen the preacher carried away with his own witticisms, thereby grieving the Spirit. The atmosphere of the gathering changed immediately into a soulish one. When we use humour, we must use it with fear and trembling.

While it is refreshing to meet a brother bubbling over with spontaneous humour, the majority of us have not this gift naturally. In "Hollywood Evangelism" I have quoted the saying of Richard Baxter: "I preached, as never sure to preach again, and as a dying man to dying men." We must weep over the perishing. Whitfield used to say, "If you won't weep for yourselves, then I will weep for you," and often he would break down with uncontrollable weeping in the pulpit. During my childhood days in Scotland, I was brought up with this old-fashioned preaching, without any of the present-day glamor type of evangelism. They were old-fashioned preachers, with a terrible burden upon them. Peter Hynd was a precious man of God, who worked in the coal mines all week and preached on the Lord's Day. With burning eloquence, he pressed home the claims of Christ. The hush of eternity was always upon the gatherings. Rarely did I ever see that preacher finish a sermon without getting down on his knees, and with tear-stained face, plead with God to save the unsaved. In our own ministry in Europe, sinners often have cried aloud in deep conviction of sin, and interrupted the message.

> Strike the stoutest sinner through,
>   Start the cry 'What must I do?'
> Make them weep, till born anew
>   Through the Lamb.

DEBATING

Think of the beautiful words concerning the Lord Jesus in Isaiah 42:3, "And a bruised reed will He not break, and a smoking flax will He not quench." Paul says, "The servant of the Lord must not strive, but be gentle unto all men, apt to teach, patient, in meekness instructing those that oppose themselves" (II Timothy 2:24-25).

The believer is a witness, not a debater. As a boy, at sixteen years of age, I fell into the snare of debating with infidel lecturers, but I very soon discovered that very few are saved by logical argument. "Preach the Word," said Paul. There is grave danger of arguing about divine truth, for arguing's sake.

Richard Weaver, commonly known as "Undaunted Dick," the co-labourer of Henry Moorehouse, the young man who revolutionized the life of D. L. Moody, was a rare exhibition of this grace of humility. His rough, rugged nature was transformed by the Spirit of God into a gracious, quiet spirit.

> I need no other argument;
> I want no other plea—
> It is enough that Jesus died,
> And that He died for me.

BOASTING OF RESULTS ACHIEVED

Again and again we have known men and movements graciously used by God, who, in their fleshly indulgence of counting numbers, and the boasting of the flesh, have grieved the Spirit. Read the heart-breaking story of David's sin in I Chronicles 21. What the Philistines, the Ammonites, and the Syrians failed to effect, the devil accomplished through pride. After a victory, there is always a secret temptation in the heart of a Christian to search for a personal and carnal cause. David, in his pride, fell into Satan's snare. Had he obeyed the Scripture, the foundation of the Temple would have been laid, as that of the Tabernacle was, with the redemption money of the thousands of Israel, instead of the blood of the seventy thousand that perished. How we all love our statistics! Because of the advance of science in radio and television, there never was such a time in the history of the Church when the results were so advertised as today. Hundreds of Christian magazines are dedicated to this one purpose; to boast over results achieved. Evangelistic parties have paid publicity agents for this purpose. Evangelical news-writers are itching to write of wonderful accomplishments in the field of evangelism. How dangerous and deadly is our sin of counting numbers.

So great is the craze of advertising man in his accomplishments, that it is almost impossible now for an evangelist or missionary quietly and humbly to testify to God's blessing upon his ministry. There is verily a place in our Christian publications for a quiet, conservative report of the "sound of a going in the tops of the mulberry trees" (II Sam. 5:24), but that is something vastly different from our custom of magnifying man and movements. We write pages about the instruments and their personalities, but very little about the Blesser.

I believe we must testify to what God has done when we have the permission of the Spirit so to do. Even then, we must plead the covering of the precious blood of the Lord Jesus. In Leviticus 2:1-13 we have the various ingredients of the meal offering described. The frankincense represented the fragrance of the life of Christ Godward, and refers to our devotion and worship. All the frankincense must be burned and the fragrance of it wafted back to God. None of it belongs to us. We are to take no glory unto ourselves. The late Miss Ruth Paxson used to pray, "O Lord, do not even let me touch Thy glory!"

If it is man's doing, then let us praise man for the power of his accomplishments, but if we can truly say, "This is the Lord's doing; it is marvellous in our eyes" (Psa. 118:23), then let us give God all the glory.

THE EXAGGERATION OF THE TRUTH

How tragic that we can laugh at the phrase, "evangelically speaking," meaning that this is slightly more than the bare facts. Many times in the excitement of a meeting, or speaking extemporaneously, we may make a mistake in quoting facts and figures, but to do so wilfully grieves the Spirit. Sir Winston Churchill, during World War II, had to gather the Royal Air Force pilots to a briefing session. He said to them: "In your eagerness and sincerity to die for the Empire and win the war, you are in danger of losing it for us, because of exaggerating the truth. We have been depending on the accuracy of your statements after your flights, at the briefing sessions, but we have discovered that many times not so many planes were shot down, and not so many war targets were bombed as reported. Please, gentlemen, be as factual and accurate in your figures as possible."

How necessary it is in our missionary and evangelistic reports, that we stick close to facts, or else through giving false information we can lose the spiritual war. How many times during the past twenty years we have evangelized Europe and the world — on paper only! Sometimes after the smoke of the battle is cleared away, we find that we did not conquer so much after all.

SELF RELIANCE

Oh, how cunning is Satan and how subtle is the flesh! Peter and Samson fell because of self-reliance. How easy it is to lean upon past experiences; how easy it is to carry on in our own strength and energy, after the right hand of God has been upon us! We cannot stand against the onslaughts of hell for one single moment, apart from the power of Christ. In our own strength we cannot win even one soul for Christ.

WORRY

The habit of worry is another great waste of divine power. Worry is a great sin. If you worry, you do not trust; and if you trust, you do not worry. How many believers worry over the fruits of their labours, instead of leaving the increase with God. Sometimes, like that

143

of the prophets, our message is doomed to failure at the outset. Sometimes we have to be a "savour of death unto death" as well as the "savour of life unto life" (II Cor. 2:16). If we have no sin in our lives, and have preached the glorious Gospel with the "Holy Ghost sent down from heaven," we may safely leave the results with God. "So shall My Word be, that goeth forth out My mouth: it shall not return unto Me void, but it shall accomplish that which I please, and it shall prosper in the thing whereto I sent it" (Isa. 55:11). Sometimes when we see no apparent results, these are the most fruitful periods of our ministry.

How many lose the peace and joy and glory in their souls, because they have that deep gnawing fear that God has failed them. They say that they are trusting God, and yet they have already made preparations for the possibility of God failing them. Some people, instead of drowning their troubles, take them out and give them swimming exercises! Some people worry because they have nothing to worry about.

John Wesley once stood out very nobly in disregarding the eyes of men, so long as he stood acquitted in the eyes of God. Among his many persecutions is to be numbered the falling back of former friends, including his wife. These turned against him and published many spiteful things, even defaming his character in a shocking manner. Brother Charles hastened off in alarm and indignation to find out what defence brother John would set up. There was no time to lose! The eyes of the world were upon him, and God's enemies and his own would be glad to make capital out of so contemptible a business! What was Charles' surprise to find that John was resolved in doing simply nothing! The great preacher was calm and comfortable in mind, being entirely free from any concern in the matter. Yes,

he was trusting in the promise of God, "No weapon
that is formed against thee shall prosper; and every
tongue that shall rise against thee in judgment, thou
shalt condemn. This is the heritage of the servants of
the Lord, and their righteousness is of Me, saith the
Lord" (Isa. 54;17).

DISCOURAGEMENT

The Christian is in most danger of a deep fall immediately after a great triumph. We should be especially watchful and prayerful immediately after great
times of blessing. Elijah could boldly face the four
hundred.prophets of Baal, but he fled for his life next
day from one woman. "He went for his life." Accompanied by his servant and under cover of darkness, he
hurried through the storm, across the hills of Samaria
toward the extreme south of Judea. He was utterly
demoralized and panic-stricken. The terrible reaction
which so often comes to us after some tremendous ten-
sion and victorious battle over the enemy, seized hold
upon God's servant. Elijah grew discouraged, possibly
through a relapse of his physical powers. He was
drained dry of his physical energy. How often we all
have experienced this! Christ is saying to many a tired,
weary worker, "Take My yoke upon you, and learn of
Me; for I am meek and lowly in heart: and ye shall find
rest unto your souls, for My yoke is easy and My burden
is light" (Matt. 11:28-30). To avoid such periods of
discouragement, we must "come apart and rest awhile"
with our glorious Redeemer. It is the rested workers
that God wants.

Angry and rebellious, the prophet crawled into a
cave. Are you in a cave, tired, wearied and discouraged?
Then the voice of God comes to you as to His servant,

145

"What doest thou here, Elijah?"

Discouragement gets us out of touch with God. Discouragement gets us out of the line of God's will. Discouragement gives us wrong thoughts of our loving Father. Says Robert Murray McCheyne, "If I could hear Christ praying for me in the next room I would not fear a million enemies. Yet the distance makes no difference. He IS praying for me!"

PAMPERING THE FLESH

There are four great sins mentioned in the New Testament, all of which are in relation to the human body: the sin of gluttony, the sin of drunkenness, the sin of murder, and the sin of impurity. Paul in his epistles lays great emphasis on the believer's body, as for instance in Romans 12:1, "Present your bodies a living sacrifice," and I Cor. 6:20, "For ye are bought with a price; therefore glorify God in your body and in your spirit, which are God's." In the life of that great pioneer missionary to China, Dr. Timothy Richards, his biographer tells us of a very striking incident. Dr. Richards had given to an educated, cultured Chinese gentleman a copy of the New Testament, and this gentleman promised to read it. When he met Dr. Richards again, he said, "I have read the New Testament through as I promised."

"Well," said the doctor, "what was the deepest impression made upon your mind in reading the New Testament?"

To the missionary's surprise, he replied, "The wonderful truth that the body may be the temple of the Holy Spirit."

Surely that pagan gentleman recognized the glory and the mystery of the Christian life.

Have you been ignoring the claims of Christ upon

146

your body? Have you been grieving the Holy Spirit through sins in the body? Many believers have a wastage of spiritual power because they have not brought their bodies under subjection to the Holy Spirit. It is often surprising to see so many so-called spiritual believers impair the health of the body, which is the instrument of the Lord, by over-indulgence in eating and drinking.

HANDLING SACRED MATTERS IN A FAMILIAR WAY

One of Samson's great sins was that of becoming familiar with divine realities. Samson lost the Shekinah glory because he lost the sanctity of his Nazarite position. He became accustomed to being a holy instrument of God (Numbers 6). How easy it is to become accustomed to sacred things in the Lord's work! How easy it is to lose the thrill and glory of the Christian life! Do you remember the "days of your youth?" (Hosea 2:15). Do you remember with what holy reverence and awe you first bowed your neck to the yoke of Christ? You remember "your first love" and the glorious communion with the risen Redeemer! Has the glory of your sacred "high-calling of God in Christ Jesus" ceased to thrill your soul? (Phil. 3:14).

The devil hates reverence. One of his great objectives is to destroy the spirit of reverence and awe from among the flock of God. What a tragedy that sometimes the Roman Catholics and Greek Orthodox have a greater reverence for the Name of our blessed Lord than we Evangelicals! It seems that some Christian leaders make it the ambition of their lives to explain away and do away with all the mystery and sacredness of this glorious supernatural life. "Back-slapping," and frivolous

147

song leaders, and masters of ceremony, have reduced our evangelical fundamental Christianity to the same level as a football pep session and auctioneer show. Some services are nothing more than a glorified spiritual vaudeville! Some have even sunk so low as to throw around in a joking manner in song services the majestic Messianic title of Christ, "Amen." ("These things saith the Amen, the faithful and true witness, and beginning of the creation of God" Rev. 3:14.) They have changed the Spirit-exalting, awe-inspiring cries of "hallelujah" into cheap usage for laughing and joking. How solemn, sacred, majestic and glorious is the use of the word "Hallelujah" in the book of Revelation (Rev. 1:6-7, 18; 3:14; 5:14; 7:12; 19:4; 22:20).

Where there is no heavenly awe, there is no heavenly blessing.

FAILURE TO TESTIFY OF
BLESSING RECEIVED

Have you had a glorious time with the Lord, when He has flooded your soul with His peace and power? It may be the Lord gave you a glorious experience in times of deep testing, or gave you a fresh nugget from the gold mine of His Word. Have you testified to the Lord's goodness? "Let the redeemed of the Lord say so!" (Psa. 107:2). If you do not testify, then you can easily lose the blessing. Satan hates the quiet, humble testimony of the saints to the Lord's goodness. The Psalmist cried out, "My soul shall make her boast in the Lord: the humble shall hear thereof and be glad. O mangnify the Lord with me, and let us exalt His Name together. I sought the Lord, and He heard me, and delivered me from all my fears. . . . O taste and see that the Lord is good: blessed is the man that trusteth in Him" (Psa. 34:2-4,8).

Even saintly men like Fletcher of Madeley have lost tremendous experiences with the Lord because of failure to humbly testify. Sometimes we are afraid to testify because the carnal believers will think we are foolish or immodest. The Maréchale says, "Nothing fills all hell with dismay like a reckless, dare-devil, shouting faith."

FAILURE TO WALK IN REVEALED LIGHT

It is only as we keep walking in the light already given that God will give us more light. A young Salvation Army lassie in Great Britain was asked the secret of her radiant, vigorous witness. Said she, "It is simple. I walk in the light of God's revealed truth to me, and in that walk I have deliverance." "But if we walk in the light (not according to), as He is in the light, we have fellowship one with another, and the blood of Jesus Christ, His Son cleanseth us from all sin" (I John 1:7).

You see, the more light the Holy Spirit gives us, the more obedience there must be. "Power belongeth unto God," and He bestows His power on His own terms, and one of the conditions is obedience. "The Holy Ghost, Whom God hath given to them that obey Him" (Acts 5:32). It is true that dedication brings us to the threshhold of the Spirit-filled life, but for the constant manifestation of power, there must be a maintained attitude of obedience. Dedication is more than an act; it is an attitude.

Sometimes there is disobedience to God's plan and place of service. We map out our own plan and place of service and are disobedient to the heavenly vision and call. A missionary must be willing to do anything on the mission field for Christ's sake. If God's will is for you to be a "nobody"—misunderstood, working in an

149

insignificant position while others are being glamorized —you must be quiet before the Lord. If the Spirit places you in a difficult sphere to do a sowing ministry, while others have a reaping ministry, you must obey with joy.

FAILURE TO WATCH AND PRAY

Many of us have a "leakage of divine power" because we do not watch and pray (Matt. 26:41). The disciples miserably denied the Lord and got out of fellowship with Him in the hallowed spot of Gethsemane. They were fast asleep at the time the Lord needed them most. They failed to watch and pray.

Why is it that oft-times it is the deeply spiritual man or woman that has the greatest fall? The reason is obvious; the higher you climb, the greater the fall! The Alpine guides of Switzerland will tell you that they do not have many accidents on the lower parts of the Matterhorn; the majority of the accidents take place on the higher heights of this great mountain, because the climbers get more careless the higher they ascend. So it is in the spiritual realm. In the rare atmosphere of the mountains of communion and spiritual intimacy there is a grave danger of the presumption of self-reliance.

William Booth used to say in his officers' councils, "Take time to pray God's blessing down in your soul every day. If you do not, you will lose God. God is leaving men every day. They once had power. They walked in the glorious strength of God, but they ceased to wait on Him and earnestly seek His face. I am a very busy man, but I take time to get alone with God every day to commune with Him."

What a tragedy when the Shekinah glory departs because of neglect!

FAILURE DURING TIMES OF TESTING

Julius Sturn has written these blessed words:

Pain's furnace-heat within me quivers,
God's breath upon the flame doth blow;
And all my heart in anguish shivers
And trembles at the fiery glow:
And yet I whisper: "As God will!"
And in His hottest fire stand still.

He comes, and lays my heart, all heated,
On the hard anvil, minded so
Into His own fair shape to beat it
With His great hammer, blow on blow:
And yet I whisper: "As God will!"
And at His heaviest blows hold still.

He takes my softened heart and beats it;
The sparks fly off at every blow;
He turns it o'er and o'er and heats it,
And lets it cool and makes it glow.
And yet I whisper: "As God will!"
And in His mighty hand hold still.

Why should I murmur? For the sorrow
Thus only long-lived would be;
Its end may come, and will tomorrow,
When God has done His work in me.
So I say trusting: "As God will!"
And trusting to the end hold still.

He kindles for my profit purely,
Affliction's glowing fiery brand;
And all His heaviest blows are surely
Inflicted by a Master's hand:
So I say praising: "As God will!"
And hope in Him, and suffer still.

151

FAILURE TO CO-OPERATE WITH GOD

The ministry of the prophet Jonah gives us an insight into the frailty of human nature. Jonah was out of fellowship with the great heart of God concerning the salvation of a heathen nation. The word of the Lord had to come unto him "a second time" (Jonah 3:1). There was not a single word of reproach; simply a renewed commission—a second chance. This time Jonah obeyed, but he was still out of fellowship with his Master in His great plan and purpose. Like Elijah under the juniper tree, Jonah under the sheltering gourd, full of self-pity and touchiness, was angry with God. Once again in tenderness, Jehovah asked the searching question, "Doest thou well to be angry?" Jonah was angry for the fate of the gourd, and yet desired the destruction of a whole city! The story ends with God's final challenge to Jonah, vindicating His own righteousness and exposing Jonah's inconsistency. How many times we see ourselves reflected in Jonah! Oh for grace to enter into fellowship with all God's plans and purposes for perishing humanity!

FAILURE TO RECEIVE FRESH RENEWALS
OF THE HOLY SPIRIT

The Christian life is one of continuous abiding. "As the branch cannot bear fruit of itself, except it abide in the vine; no more can ye except ye abide in Me" (John 15:4). Says blessed McCheyne, "It is the look that saves, but it is the gaze that sanctifies." If we would maintain the life of power and peace and spiritual prosperity, we must draw daily from the Throne of Grace and from the Word of God.

George Muller tells us, "The first three years after conversion I neglected the Word of God. Since I began to search it diligently, the blessing has been wonderful. I have read the Bible through one hundred times, and always with increasing delight. I look upon it as a lost day when I have not had a good time over the Word of God. Friends often say, 'I have so much to do, so many people to see, that I cannot find time for Scripture study.' Perhaps there are not many who have more to do than I have, for more than half a century I have never known one day when I have not had more business than I could get through. For forty years I have had annually about thirty thousand letters, and most of these have passed through my own hands.* I have nine assistant's always at work corresponding in several languages. Then, as pastor of a church with twelve hundred believers, great has been my care. Besides, I have had charge of five immense orphanages; also at my publishing depot, the printing and circulation of millions of tracts, books, and Bibles. But I have always made it a rule never to begin work until I have had a good season with God. The vigour of our spiritual life will be in exact proportion to the place held by the Word in our lives and thoughts."

Erasmus, in his introduction to the Greek New Testament of 1516, says of the Scriptures, "They will give Christ to you in an intimacy so close that He would be less visible to you if He stood before your eyes."

The keen Bible student will notice the striking similarity between Ephesians 5:18 and Colossians 3:16. The result of the Word's indwelling is the same as that of the Spirit's indwelling. There is no once-and-for-all baptism for power that ignores daily renewals (Titus 3:5).

Finney spoke about receiving many baptisms of the Spirit. Some brethren would prefer to call these ex-

*No typewriters then! (J.A.S.)

periences "special anointings." When we study the history of the early church, we find that they prayed and received mighty renewals after times of great conflict and persecution. "And when they had prayed, the place was shaken where they were assembled together; and they were all filled with the Holy Ghost, and they spoke the Word of God with boldness" (Acts 4:31).

We believe that these disciples were not guilty of any unfaithfulness, nor had they neglected any of the ministries of grace. As John Bunyan might say, "They had used up their spending money, and had need to repair to the Bank of Heaven for fresh supplies." As one may become physically exhausted, so one may be spiritually spent. Thus one needs renewals of divine power.

In Europe we love to gather the believers in order that we may wait in the presence of God for the heavenly descending dew (Hosea 14:5). Dr. Scofield tells of a sacred experience of his. He heard an Irish preacher speak on Naaman the leper. The preacher and the message were very lifeless. As Dr. Scofield left the church with another brother, his companion whispered to him, "That dear man needs a fresh dip in the Jordan." The noted Bible expositor says, "I excused myself and went out into the country and into the night. I looked up at the stars and I cried to God with the tears running down my cheeks, "O God, I am the man who needs the fresh dip in Jordan!" God met Dr. Scofield there. May God help us to have these fresh renewals alone with Himself!

In closing, may I say there are many other ways whereby we may lose this baptism of power (Luke 24:49). There may be a leakage through the reading of novels, through allowing sporting events to become first in our interests, and through other seemingly harmless pastimes. I once read of a Salvation Army officer

154

who used to go an hour earlier to the hall to pray for God's mighty blessing. Gradually he came to spend this time playing dreamy sentimental music on his violin, and within a year he had lost out with God.

That blessed man of God, James Caughey, who won General William Booth to Christ, and who was so greatly used of God on both sides of the Atlantic, tells in one of his books how he was invited out to tea one evening, and though there was nothing harmful in the talk of the hour, he discovered as he went into the meeting that night his soul was like a loosely-strung bow. He could not shoot the King's arrows into the hearts of the King's enemies, for he had no power. It had been lost at the tea-table!

One cannot criticize another. Before our own Master we stand or fall. What may affect one life may not affect another. Let us "guard our deposits," as Paul instructed young Timothy. Let us "keep the securities of the faith intact" (I Timothy 6:20).

Let us bow in prayer as we lay aside this book, and ask God to speak to us in the stillness.

A WORD TO BACKSLIDERS

The Word of God is full of comfort and consolation to the backslider. The prophecies of Jeremiah and Hosea have a special message for the backslider. In Hosea, chapter two, we have God in His tenderness, seeking to chastise an adulterous Israel and bring her back to Himself. "Therefore, behold I will allure her, and bring her into the wilderness, and speak comfortably unto her. And I will give her vineyards from thence, and the valley of Achor for a door of hope: and she shall sing there, as in the days of her youth, and as in the day when she came out from the land of Egypt" (Hosea 2:14-15).

"I will heal their backsliding, I will love them freely: for mine anger is turned away from him. . . . Ephraim shall say, What have I to do any more with idols? I have heard Him and observed him" (Hosea 14:4-8).

Hast thou heard Him, seen Him, known Him,
　　Is not thine a captured heart?
Chief among ten thousand own Him,
　　Gladly choose the better part.

What has stript the seeming beauty
　　From the idols of the earth?
Not the sense of right or duty,
　　But the sight of peerless worth.

Not the crushing of the idols,
　　With its bitter void and smart,
But the beaming of His beauty
　　The unveiling of His heart.

'Tis that look that melted Peter,
　　'Tis that face that Stephen saw,
'Tis that heart that wept with Mary,
　　Can alone from idols draw—

Draw, and win, and fill completely,
　　Till the cup o'erflows the brim;
What have we to do with idols,
　　Who have companied with Him?

A BENEDICTION

May the love of a dying Saviour, the power of a risen Saviour, the intercession of an ascended Saviour, and the glory of a returning Saviour, be the comfort and hope of all our hearts!

Ten

Why so Few Believers are Filled With the Spirit

"It costs much to obtain the power of the Spirit: it costs self-surrender and humiliation and a yielding up of our most precious things to God; it costs the perseverence of long waiting, and the faith of strong trusts. But when we are really in that power, we shall find this difference, that whereas before, it was hard for us to do the easiest things, now it is easy for us to do the hard things." *A. J. Gordon*

"Many want the Spirit's power but not the Spirit's purity. The Holy Spirit does not rent out His attributes. His power is never separated from His glorious Self."   *J. A. S.*

"IF A SON SHALL ASK BREAD OF ANY OF you that is a father, will he give him a stone? Or if he ask a fish, will he for a fish give him a serpent? Or if he ask an egg, will he offer him a scorpion? If ye then, being evil, know how to give good gifts unto your children; how much more shall your heavenly Father give the Holy Spirit to them that ask Him" (Luke 11:11-13).

A calm survey of the evangelical world today would lead one to conclude that very few believers are full of the Holy Ghost. Earnest workers in the Lord's cause may be numbered by tens of thousands, yet only a small number of these would profess to enjoy this vital relationship with their Lord. We are well aware that the Saviour's promise as found in the eleventh chapter of Luke's Gospel was spoken before Pentecost, but we would remind our readers that it was recorded after Pentecost. We believe that this Scripture gives us encouragement to pray for an even greater fulness of the already indwelling Spirit. Many have claimed this precious promise, and yet are baffled and perplexed because their cry is apparently unheeded. May we suggest some reasons why they have not experienced the blessing they have sought:

NOT READY

I believe the paramount reason why many believers are not filled with the Spirit is that they are not ready to receive this priceless blessing from God. Either they do not know what it is they ask, or they have not submitted themselves to God's preliminary dealings with them. The gift of the Fulness is the greatest blessing that can come to a child of God. God is not going to give His choicest of blessings to one who has not in some measure a real appreciation of the glory of the blessing, as the Holy Spirit is so wonderful! How many believers pray glibly: "Oh God, fill me with Thy Spirit." The superficiality of their prayer is an open witness to the fact that they have no true realization of the grandeur of such a blessing. It is seemingly a mere repetition of evangelical phraseology.

If it were possible to conceive that God, in His infinite mercy, would give the Holy Spirit in His fulness to those who are not ready to receive Him, the experience would prove a grave danger. How many times have you, as a parent, given a costly present to your precious child, only to discover that he was too immature to appreciate the value of it. Again, would you give your child your valuable watch to play with, just because he asked you for it? No! you would be afraid that he would misuse it because he is not yet ready to receive it. In the spiritual realm, think of Paul having to receive "a thorn in the flesh" to keep him humble. "And lest I should be exalted above measure, through the abundance of the revelations, there was given to me a thorn in the flesh, the messenger of Satan to buffet me, lest I should be exalted above measure" (II Cor. 12:7). If the mighty apostle was in danger of becoming conceited through the glory of his spiritual experiences, how much more are we! But God, in His infinite mercy and wisdom does not give us the fulness of blessing until He knows we are ready to receive it.

WRONG MOTIVE

Another reason why so few receive the fulness of the Spirit is that many are not seeking Him with the right motive. In that deep, spiritual, though neglected epistle of James, we have a very practical word: "Ye ask, and receive not, because ye ask amiss, that ye may consume it upon your own lusts" (James 4:3). How often self mingles in a subtle way with the cry of the soul! The word "lusts" means "that ye may spend it in your own pleasures." How many times our so-called noble desires are filled with fleshly ambitions. Sometimes we want to be filled with the Spirit for self-exaltation. We want to be mightily used of God in order that our name might appear prominently in Christian magazines. We want to talk about our converts and our great successful campaigns, so that we can bask in the sunshine of the admiration of the saints. How often there is a desire for "unction" in our preaching, in order that thousands will listen to our message, and that cities will fall prostrate before us, like the city of Jericho, at the sound of a trumpet voice! In others, again, it is for the power of being used instrumentally to bring vast numbers to Christ which inspires them to ask for the blessing. In many ways this is a noble desire; yet how subtle and all but overpowering the temptation which lurks in it!

Oh dear brother and sister, God will not give the Spirit to glorify us or to promote any of our causes, that we might spend the blessing on our own self-gratification. Many want the Spirit's power, but not the Spirit's purity. The Holy Spirit does not rent out His attributes. His power is never separated from His glorious Self. The Spirit of power is the Spirit of holiness.

Others selfishly seek His fulness for the sake of having the experience; in other words, for the sake of joy, peace, and spiritual ecstasy, or merely for their own personal benefit.

How few souls there are whom God can trust with such a power!

NOT PREPARED FOR THE RESULTS

Looking at the thought from another aspect, we would say that many do not have their prayer answered because the Father knows they are not prepared for the possible consequences of being filled with the Spirit. They are seeking the fulness on their own terms. Pastor A. Douglas Brown tells of God's mighty and faithful dealings with him when a successful shepherd of a London church. God was preparing him to be an instrument for revival in the churches of Britain; an instrument for bringing thousands to Christ. He wanted God's best, but he definitely was not willing to pay God's price. He wanted God to use him on Douglas Brown's terms. After four months of battle, he lay broken and empty at the foot of the Cross. When telling the story of that experience he refers to the patience of God: "God is very patient. It took Him four months to teach me to say two words: 'Lord, anything'."

I am reminded of four outstanding men in the Bible of whom we are told that they were filled with the Spirit: John the Baptist (Luke 1:15), Stephen (Acts 6:5), Peter (Acts 4:8), and Barnabas (Acts 11:24). The consequences of their fulness was not the same in their lives and ministry. Stephen did not convert the Sanhedrin by the force of his mighty sermon. They did not tremble before him as he spoke: nor did he melt them into tears. He only intensified their opposition, so that they stoned him as a blasphemer. On the other hand, Peter, filled with the Holy Ghost, preached the same Gospel and three thousand souls were won to Christ. John the Baptist preached only six months. Barnabas was commanded by the Spirit to sell his property for the Lord's work.

The results of being filled with the Spirit are not uniform. The life and work of William C. Burns is to my mind one of the most eloquent illustrations of our study. After graduating at an early age from Glasgow University, he became the mightiest evangelist in Scotland at the age of twenty-two years. Spiritual giants, like Andrew and Horatio Bonar, Murray McCheyne, John Milne, R. S. Candlish, and a host of others, sat at his feet like little children, in the realm of evangelistic work. After some five years of revival in his native land, the Holy Ghost sent him to pagan China as a foreign missionary, where he laboured for the rest of his life in comparative obscurity. Hudson Taylor and other Chinese missionaries could testify that William C. Burns, the missionary, was just as full of the Holy Ghost as William C. Burns, the evangelist! One often ponders this mystery, of why a man who is leading thousands to Christ, should be led by the Spirit to leave such a mighty, successful ministry for a less prominent one, and to learn a new language "to preach the unsearchable riches of Christ." However, we remember the instance in the Acts of how Philip was taken from the revival in the city of Samaria to go into the desert to win one soul for Christ.

Again, we are reminded of how Paul received the fulness of the Spirit at the very threshold of his new life in Christ (Acts 9:17), and yet he did not go up to Jerusalem to preach to thousands. On the contrary, he was led by the Spirit to go into Arabia where he remained for three years, preaching to nobody! (Gal. 1:15-18). Arabia was Paul's theological seminary! This is where the Spirit taught him the deep, spiritual truths of the Word of God. Thus we see that the life that is fully possessed by the Spirit is not always an actively successful public life. As in the case of "Praying Hyde" and Father Nash, it may be a life of isolation from the Christian public for the ministry of intercession.

We cannot dictate to the Holy Spirit. We cannot lay down what we think should be the avenues of our service. Personally, I cannot tell you what will be the consequences of your fulness, but one thing I do know from experience, it will be a life of constant sacrifice for the Person and work of our blessed Lord. Are you prepared, like John the Baptist, to have only six months of ministry, and then imprisonment, only to have your head chopped off at the end of it? Are you prepared, like Stephen, to thunder forth the message of God in such a manner that your congregation will hate you to the gnashing of their teeth and the stoning you out of the ministry? Are you prepared like Barnabas, to obey the voice of the Spirit and sell your possessions as well as giving yourself to the Lord? We had the joy once of leading a dear business man in Europe into the experience of the Fulness. Within a week the Spirit had told him to give several thousands of dollars for the work of the Lord. Are you prepared, dear father and mother, that the Holy Spirit should take your children for foreign mission work? Are you prepared, dear young couple, to be lonely sentinels of the Cross of Christ on the mission field?

In a word, the terms on which God is prepared to give this most peerless gift to a believer are that the life shall be absolutely at God's own disposal, as He has purposed after the counsel of His own will (Ephes. 1:11).

SIN AND DOUBTFUL INDULGENCES

The Holy Spirit will not fill a dirty vessel, even as the mother in the kitchen will not fill an unclean vessel. It is sheer blasphemy to ask God to fill you with the Holy Spirit while you are living in sin and disobedience to the revealed will of God. It is quite easy to pray, "Oh God, fill me with Thy Spirit," but it is another thing to deal with the sin which is wrong in the life. William Booth said to his fighting soldiers, "Before we go to our knees to receive the baptism of fire, let me beg of you to see to it that your souls are in harmony with the will and purpose of the Holy Spirit, Whom you seek. See to it that the channel of communication, by which the baptism of the Holy Spirit must be received, be kept open. I heard of some people the other day who could not get any water. They turned the tap repeatedly, but no water came. They sent to the office of the company, who sent a man to examine the connections and the fittings, but all was right. Plenty of water in the reservoir; pipes, taps, and connections all right, but no water. At last they pulled up the pipe and found a mouse in it. It is no use turning the tap—praying, singing or even believing—if there is something you are holding back or refusing to do, some idol, something about which you feel condemned, but which you refuse to give up; something in the pipe. Perhaps it is some trumpery, contemptible thing. Out with it; give it no rest; give it up.

Destroy your idols and hindrances and stoppages with an everlasting destruction. Let there be free communication between you and God. Let all go, and you shall be flooded before you rise from your knees; the world shall feel the power of it and God shall have all the glory."

Doubtful indulgences can also keep us back from the blessing. Paul says, "All things are lawful unto me, but all things are not expedient; all things are lawful unto me, but I will not be brought under the power of any." (I Cor. 6:12). There may be some things in your life which are not sin, but which are certainly "weights" (Heb. 12:1), which hinder the Spirit from taking full control. At a Holiness Convention several years ago in Britain, a harrassed believer came with a broken heart to the chairman. "Oh sir," he cried, "I cannot be filled with the Spirit, because if I gave up my indulgence, then I would die!" "Then," said the chairman, unsparingly, "Then just die, my brother." If I want God's best, I must give Him my best. Even legitimate things must go at His command. Before I can receive one hundred per cent from Christ, I must be one hundred per cent for Christ.

SOCIAL LIFE

Sometimes our very social life can be the hinderance to our being filled with the Spirit. We have reached a very high standard of civilization; God has prospered us and given us beautiful, comfortable homes. Therein lies the snare. Our blessings have become a curse, through selfish usage. Too many believers engage in such a busy social life that they have neither time nor disposition to be occupied with the Spirit of God. They have become earthly-minded. Their life is one round of constant social whirl—not sinful in itself, except that it leaves little time for heart-searching, intercession, Bible study, and waiting quietly with the Lord. We well remember how, during the Christmas season, in a European country, the believers were so busy "coffee drinking" from house to house that the whole Christmas services were void of spiritual unction. (By the same principle, we have known many churches to miss God's best in special conferences and campaigns, because the Bible teacher or evangelist had to spend so much time in the believers' homes for meals. I have often told a pastor, "I love the fellowship of the saints. I would like to have a meal in every home of your congregation, but I am not here for a social life; I am here to deliver God's message. Please do not accept too many invitations for me among your people for a social time, otherwise I will have too little time to be alone with God.")

Now I say that next to knowing Christ as Lord, the greatest joy is to know and have fellowship with our fellow believers. The danger comes when our fellowship consists of nothing more than eating and drinking and empty talk. The Scriptures lay down the principle in this matter: "Whether therefore ye eat or drink, or whatsoever ye do, do all to the glory of God" (I Cor. 10:31). We know of a dear sister who endeavours on every occasion during social fellowship with believers, to turn the conversation to the Christ of God, that the gathering might be edifying.

My brother, my sister, do you know your Bible well enough that you don't need to study it any more? Have you graduated in your prayer life, that you do not need to spend any more hours in prayer? The lonely missionary has little social contact in his isolation as a servant of the Lord. Sometimes the only social life he

167

has is through reading the letters from home. Are you willing, as God reveals to you, to give up some of your social life in order to have time alone with God?

> Not many lives, but only one have we—
> One, only one;
> How sacred should that one life ever be—
> That narrow span!
> Day after day filled up with blessed toil,
> Hour after hour still bringing in new spoil.

NOT THIRSTING

"If any man thirst," our Lord said, "let him come unto Me and drink." It is only when a believer is so thirsty that he is willing to give up everything that would hinder him from being filled with the Spirit, that he receives the fulness. Said one believer to another, "I would give the world to have your experience with the Lord." "That is what it cost me," replied the other.

A lady missionary on the West coast of Africa spoke in the mood of quiet witness to Sammy Morris about the Holy Spirit. The soul of the young Kru convert was enthused about the Gift Divine, and he regularly walked miles to the mission-school in order to hear more about Pentecost. Time and again the missionary told the story of the Spirit's coming, and made her witness. At last, wearied of the repetition, she said, "If you want to know more, you must go and see Stephen Merritt. He told me all I know of the Holy Spirit." "Where is he?" "In New York," she laughingly replied. A few days afterwards they missed him. He had gone to New York to find Stephen Merritt, and to hear about the fulness of the Holy Spirit. It is a beautiful spiritual romance. He walked weary miles to the coast and pleaded for days with the captain of a ship to allow him to work his passage to New York. He slept on the sand till permission was given. Aboard the vessel he suffered terrible persecution; but in the end he triumphed in the Lord. One day he was sent to clean the captain's cabin. They found him pointing the captain to Christ. The sacred flame of conviction spread throughout the ship. Several men were converted. Arriving at New York, Sammy found Stephen Merritt just as the good man was leaving his home for a service. "Are you Stephen Merritt? . . . I am Sammy Morris. I've just come from Africa to talk with you about the Holy Ghost." All the way from Africa to learn about the Spirit! The Gift Divine could not be denied to desire so fervent and sacrificial. Sammy received the Spirit and became a mighty apostle for Christ. He did not live long. The climate was too rigorous for him. One day in May he went fearlessly and radiantly to Jesus; but when they buried Sammy, Berry Street Church was crowded and a multitude stood outside. It was all in the power of the Spirit; and that day God called many to give their lives for Sammy's native land. This is what is meant by "wanting" the Spirit.

I remember when I was only a young believer of fourteen years of age, how the Holy Spirit made me thirsty for a richer, deeper, fuller experience of the Lord Jesus, as outlined in Ephesians 3:16-19, and how many an older believer in the faith sought to dampen my ardour. My hungry heart cried, "Oh God, I want everything Thou hast for me. I do not know all that is involved, but Oh God, lead me into Thy fulness." While my companions were playing football and other sports, I spent hours in prayer, thirsting after God. In His faithfulness, God met with me in a glorious way, and filled every longing of my soul. Oh, dear believer, are you thirsting? Oh that you may be able to pray the prayer that saintly Murray McCheyne prayed, "Oh God, make me as holy as it is possible for a saved sinner to be this side of eternity." You cannot pray a better prayer than that.

> I hunger and I thirst;
>> Jesus my Manna be:
> Ye living waters, burst
>> Out of the Rock for me!

Eleven

Resisting the Spirit

"Whenever He is thwarted, whenever He is disobeyed, whenever He gives some new revelation of Christ which brings no response, He is grieved. Alas! How often the Holy Spirit has brought some new vision of the Master that has made demands upon our devotion and loyalty to Christ and we have resisted His ministry to and through us."

J. A. S.

"It is very touching and solemn that while the Holy Ghost might, in the exercise of His omnipotence, coerce our will, and compel us to submit to His authority, yet He approaches us with the most deferential regard of our feelings and independence, even suffering us to resist and disobey Him, and bearing long with our wilfulness and waywardness."

"Behold," saith the Prince to Mansoul, "My love and care towards you. I have added to all that is past this mercy to appoint you preachers a most noble Secretary to teach you in all sublime mysteries. Take heed that you do not grieve this Minister, for if you do, He may fight against you and that will distress you more than if twelve legions should descend from My Father's court to make war upon you."   *John Bunyan* "Holy War"

J UST AS IT IS POSSIBLE FOR A BELIEVER to lie to the Holy Ghost, so it is possible for a believer to resist the Holy Ghost. It is the Spirit's ministry to lead every child of God into a deeper and richer experience with his risen Lord. He is jealous for the honour and glory of the Redeemer. He ever fights for the supremacy of Christ in our hearts and lives.

In my early Christian life I believed and taught that it is not possible for a believer to resist the Holy Spirit. I was not long in the Lord's work, however, before I received a rude awakening. I was crushed and heartbroken. I joyfully went to churches to proclaim the glorious Gospel with the power of the Holy Ghost sent down from heaven, expecting that if there was to be any resistance, it would come from the unsaved. Again and again, however, I discovered that God's people were the stumbling-block to blessing (Lev. 19:14). For some reason they resisted the message of the Holy Spirit. It might have been through coldness of heart, indifference, or complacency. It sometimes was because of sin in the heart and life. I discovered that Stephen's charge to the unbelieving Jews, "Ye do always resist the Holy Ghost"

(Acts 7:51), was applicable also to a stiffnecked Church.

It is a solemn thing to note that not many years after Pentecost the risen Lord found it necessary to speak in a very special way to the local assemblies founded in Asia regarding their sin of resisting the Spirit (Rev. Chs. 2 and 3). The message to each of these churches closes with the words, "Listen, you that have ears, to the message the Spirit has for the churches" (Knox). Let us consider for a moment the message to the first assembly to whom our Lord spoke—the church at Ephesus. After giving His commendations, He added: "Yet, there is one charge I make against thee, of losing the love that was thine at first. Remember the heights from which thou hast fallen, and repent, and go back to the old ways; or else I will come to visit thee, and, when I find thee still unrepentant, will remove thy candlestick from its place" (Rev. 2:5-6 Knox).

There had been no declension in the realm of activity in the church at Ephesus. So it is today; many of the most unspiritual Christians in our churches are active, alert, and full of zeal.

There was no falling off in their love to their church. They were proud of it, sustained it, defended it, and were jealous for it. Alas, I have known the most fervent denominational loyalty existing alongside the lowest spiritual life. In our day some love their denominations and even their independent assemblies more than they love their Lord.

There was no relaxing in their attachment to the doctrine which they professed. They fought for that which was orthodox. They earnestly contended for the faith. They were willing to die for what they believed. They were like many modern churches I have known who, while fervently upholding the fundamentals of the faith, were icy and mechanical in their love for the Lord.

Along with the commendations, there was one terrible indictment from the lips of their Lord, conveyed to them by the Holy Spirit. "Yet there is one charge that I make against thee; of losing the love that was thine at first. You have resisted the ministry of the Spirit in your lives. You have not allowed Him to lead you into the deeper and richer love-life with Me; you have not obeyed His warnings of the possibility of backsliding. You have sunk so low that you do not even love Me as you did at the first!"

Their first love was the response to His first love. "We love Him because He first loved us" (I John 4:19). "Yea, I have loved thee with an everlasting love; therefore with loving kindness have I drawn thee" (Jer. 31:3). His love was first in operation; "But God, who is rich in mercy, for His great love wherewith He loved us, even when we were dead in sins. . ." (Ephes. 2:4-5). "Now when I passed by thee, and looked upon thee, behold, thy time was the time of love" (Ezek. 16:8).

> He saw me ruined by the fall,
> Yet loved me, notwithstanding all.
> To save me from my lost estate,
> His loving kindness oh how great!

Their first love was ardent and marked with all the dewy freshness of spiritual youth. "I remember thee, the kindness of thy youth, the love of thine espousals, when thou wentest after me in the wilderness, in a land that was not sown" (Jer. 2:2). As Campbell Morgan says, "You cannot define it or explain it, but you can hear it as it passes by and leaves a song floating on the air—not a regular song at a regular hour, but like the lark on a spring morning—a burst of song at a most unusual moment—and through the day. You cannot channel or organise it—it jumps over the channel and bursts forth out of any restrictions put on it."

Their first love displaced all other loves and affections. It put Him first; it went out after Him (Col. 1:18. Song of Solomon 1:4). Even the reproach of Christ was esteemed and embraced above all earthly joys or riches. The Lord's indictment against them was that they had left all this. Against the wooing of the Spirit, they had abandoned their first love. *The Church at Ephesus had a programme, but she had no passion. There she stood; strong, proud, splendidly orthodox, perfect in organization, but stiff and starched with monumental coldness.* What a tragedy! She who had rejoiced in Him as His glorious bride had lost the thrill of her relationship. *The Saviour prefers fanaticism to formalism; devotion to decorum.*

One day in Paris a lady came to see "La Maréchale" (Mrs. Booth Clibborn). She was in great sorrow. As she pressed a bottle of poison to her lips, she cried, "Maréchale, I must end my life! My husband has just told me this morning that he does not love me any more. He told me I could have his two magnificent homes and all his money, but I could not have his heart, for it had been given to another woman." Her heart was broken. But, oh my friend, how the angels must weep and how the Saviour must be grieved over the abandonment of our first love!

It is an absolute impossibility for us to lose our first love without forfeiting something. In the preaching there is not the sensitiveness to Christ's presence, the fineness of spiritual tone, the keenness of spiritual perception. A lower tone in love means a lower tone in all the realm of our spiritual life, prayer and testimony.

"Listen, you that have ears, to the message that the

Spirit has for the Churches." The crime today is that the Church is not listening; she is ignoring and resisting the voice of the Spirit. I believe that if every pastor began to preach the solemn messages of the seven epistles of the risen Lord, something extraordinary would take place. Some of their members would walk out in anger. Some would leave the church for good. There would be trouble in many churches because so many of God's people are resisting the voice of the Spirit. They have abandoned their first love and do not want to be disturbed. *I am definitely convinced in my own mind, however, that there will be no revival in any of our evangelical churches until the members are disturbed, upset, aroused, and even angry.* I never knew revival to begin anywhere until believers became offended at the Word (John 6:61). I never knew revival to begin anywhere that the smug orthodox Christians did not hate the message which disturbed them, as well as the Lord's messenger. After much fasting and intercession I have sought to deliver God's message in some churches in North America which prided themselves on their fundamental stand for the Faith. After a few messages which I had received from high heaven just for these people, I have been asked to stop the conference or campaign. My brothers and sisters in Christ who believed everything I believed, not only bitterly resented my message, but literally hated me. I had to cry out like Paul of old: "Am I therefore become your enemy, because I tell you the truth?" (Gal. 4:16). A messenger is useful only as long as his message disturbs our comfortable routine and upsets our conventions.

What is the message of the Spirit to the churches? It is threefold: Remember! Repent! Return!

Remember! Remember the heights from which thou

hast fallen. The first epistle to the Ephesians is the epistle of "Heights," while the second (Revelation 2) is the epistle of "Depths." What a tragedy! They had fallen from the heights of the heavenly places to the depths of their own backsliding! Remember! Look up and see the height from which you have fallen. Ask the Holy Ghost to show you where you were formally seated in the heavenlies in Christ. Remember the days of your espousals when you gloriously loved the Lord. Remember those precious experiences at the Throne of Grace. Remember the agony for souls you had in the days of your first love. Remember the sweet communion with those of the burning heart. Remember the days of fasting and intercession. Remember the days when the power and glory of the Lord rested continually upon you. Remember the wooing and pleadings of the Spirit when there was prompt obedience to His voice and the holy thrill of partnership with Him. Remember—until you are broken down before the Lord and cannot sleep!

Repent! It is not enough to remember. You must repent. To retrospect—to weep and pray—is not enough, unless you repent. You will only stir up the bitter dregs at the bottom of the vessel. Repent! Change your attitude to your spiritual condition and to your Lord.

Return! "Go back to the old ways." Get right with God. Deal with the sin which separated you from God. Deal with that doubtful indulgence which caused you to backslide. Smash the idol that took Christ's place. Obey the voice of the Spirit in the matter of confession and restitution. I believe it is at this point the Spirit is resisted more greatly—the humiliating act of putting things right as the Spirit guides you. Return to your original love-life with your blessed Lord. The Holy Spirit will help you. Do not resist Him any longer. Tell Him that no matter what it costs, you are prepared to go back to the blessed old ways.

Now follows the warning. "Remember . . repent . . return, or else I will come to visit thee, and when I find thee still unrepentant will remove thy candlestick from its place." Here is no idle threat. Here is judgment swift and sure. The message is urgent. There is no time for delay. We need not wait until the judgment seat of Christ to have judgment come upon us. The wrath of God can come upon us now. God can write "Ichabod" (the glory of the Lord has departed, I Sam. 4:21) over our churches now. "Behold your house is left unto you desolate" (Matt. 23:38), is not true of Jewish temples alone. Oh how many stone buildings adorn our cities today from which the candlestick has already been removed. Their history is known to Him Who walks among the golden candlesticks. "They have a name that they are living, but they are dead" (Rev. 3:1).

Along with the warning comes a word for the "Overcomer." The trouble with these local churches was that the "shortcomers" were in the majority. In these last dark days of a dying dispensation of grace, the Holy Spirit is calling out a select company from the saints of every kindred, tongue, people and nation, who will be red-hot in their devotion to Him. God is purging His Church and preparing it for revival and the coming of the Lord. Have you returned to your first love? Are you standing triumphantly as an overcomer?

In closing, let us notice the message that the Spirit has for the churches is addressed primarily to the "angel" or "messenger" of each local church. This places the pastors and Christian leaders in a very important place of responsibility. Much of the coldness and indifference in our churches today can be attributed directly to the pulpit. "Like people, like priest. . ." (Hosea

179

4:9). Andrew Murray well says, "The standard of the ministry and the standard of the life of the believers will correspond. As in the life of the Church the Spirit is known and honoured, the need of a spiritual ministry will be felt. As the ministry becomes more deeply spiritual, the tone of the church will be raised. The two act and react on each other. The demand rules the supply, but how solemn the thought that an earnest, learned and eloquent ministry is not necessarily a ministry of the Spirit."

This is not a time for preaching soothing, comforting messages to a sleeping Church. This is the time to blow the trumpet and sound out the Gospel blast, that will so disturb and infuriate the backslidden saints that they will bestir themselves and cease from their sin of resisting the Spirit. Many pastors are willing to expound the dispensational truths of Revelation, who are afraid to deliver the Spirit's ultimatum to their people, as we find it in chapters two and three. They talk about John Calvin, John Huss, and John Knox, who thundered forth the truth, while they themselves compromise with their people. How many a fundamental pastor will fight for the blessed truth of the Gospel against great opposition from without, and yet will adjust his message to the church to suit his own flock! Through unfaithful preaching "many pastors have destroyed God's vineyard" (Jer. 22:10). It would be better for them to speak directly and definitely the ultimatum of the Spirit at the price of losing their pastorates, than for them to be condemned by the Lord at the Bema. "Behold, I am against the prophets, saith the Lord, that smooth their tongues" (Jer. 23:31).

Oh, my fellow pastors, who tell the Lord in the secret place that you love Him so much that you would be willing to die for Him, are you afraid of the faces of your own congregation? Have you yourself resisted the Spirit? If so, you have broken the vows of your ordination, that you will proclaim without fear and favor the whole counsel of God. Surely you can trust your loving Father to take care of the future if you are cast out. One thing, above all others, must be kept in mind: "It is required in stewards, that a man be found faithful" (I Cor. 4:2).

> Out in the dew and cold He stands,
>   The drops of night are on His hair;
> In patient love He waits without;
>   And who, who keeps Him there?
>
> Our ear is sealed, our heart is cold,
>   And we refuse both hearth and fare;
> He speaks, we hear not: Ah, 'tis we
>   Yes, we, who keep Him there.
>
> But now no more we shut Thee out,
>   Oh Thou, the fairest of the fair:
> Come in, Thou blessed one; we will
>   No longer keep Thee there.
>
> *Andrew Bonar.*

Twelve

Four Fundamental Facts

"All of every age, who have shown by their fruits that they had the Apostolic endowment of spiritual power, came into it by an experimental reception of the Spirit not essentially different from that of the Apostles and Evangelists." *Boardman.*

"Why should we not have a perpetual Pentecost? The Holy Ghost is not withdrawn; but there are few men who are empty enough of self to go all lengths with the Holy Ghost, without diverging into the self of fanaticism." *Baxter*

I take the promised Holy Ghost
I take the gift of Pentecost
To fill me to the uttermost
I take—*HE* undertakes.

A. J. Gordon

T HE CRYING NEED TODAY IS FOR BE-
lievers who can not only lead a lost soul to the Saviour,
but who can also lead a seeking saint into the fulness of
God (Ephes. 3:19). It has been my custom in my evangelistic campaigns to seek to have one meeting each
day for the purpose of dealing with this subject. At
Bible Conferences and other gatherings, in different
parts of the world, we have dealt with hundreds of
seeking saints, and had the joy of seeing some of them
enter a new and richer life in the risen Lord. In this
connection, it cannot be too strongly stated that the
fulness of the Spirit is not something apart from Christ,
but in Him, so that in seeking His fulness, we are but
seeking to know experimentally, what is already ours
potentially (Ephes. 1:3). I have known as many as
two thousand hungry saints to remain behind for an
after meeting to listen to a quiet heart-searching talk on
this all-important theme. May I have a heart to heart
talk with you just now? Will you kneel in reverence
before the Throne of Grace and pray that God will
help you to enter into the abundant life. Remember,
the fulness of the Spirit is an integral part of the plan

of salvation: the Lord Jesus died not only that you might be saved, but that you might be filled. I would draw your attention to four fundamental facts in relation to the fulness:

WHAT GOD CLAIMS, I YIELD

The first fact is that what God claims, I must yield. There must be a definite act of consecration. At conversion, the keys of the citadel (the will), in the town of Mansoul, are placed in a moment in the hands of Emmanuel. The knee of allegiance is bent before Him. But at consecration, something more takes place; every statute book and every law is open for His inspection. Every plan is submitted to Him for approval; every room, every basement in that famous town is flung open to Him and placed at His disposal. J. H. McConkey says, "Whether long years in coming to this crisis of surrender, or reaching it at a single bound, every consecrated child of God knows that the act of yielding was the supreme step that brought him into the fulness of the closer walk with God. Your experience may have been complicated, confused, difficult to interpret; but that this act of surrender was the culmination of it all, and this fulness of the Spirit the outcome of such act— God's responsive grace to that act—all will testify."

God is asking now complete surrender from you; complete surrender of heart, will and intellect. He will show you now, if you are sincere and honest, all that He claims in your life. It is an utter impossibility for you to receive this blessing, if there is one bit of insincerity or rebellion in your heart and mind. There must be no mental reservations. It is not for you to start handing over different things in your life to God on your own initiative; it is the entire life that He claims. He not only asks for a complete surrender of the past and the present, but of all that is entailed in the future, until He calls you home to Glory. Many are in danger of an assumed dedication because they have not been thorough in the matter of surrender. They have possibly made a swift decision at a Convention meeting without having got alone with God, that He might reveal to them what is involved in this mighty step. It may take days or even weeks in the preliminary stages alone with God in the secret place, before you are able to know what His personal claims for your life are. This sometimes is because we are not in tune with God. Remember, God deals with each of us as individuals. I am often asked by seeking souls what is the exact price they must pay for this blessing. In their eagerness, some are disturbed and even annoyed, when I do not repeat to them some uniform system which they must follow. No preacher can hand out a printed formula in a professional manner to all and sundry. There is no stock answer to this question. I have learned over a period of thirty years, that only our loving heavenly Father can reveal to us the entire cost of consecration. I cannot tell you the price you must pay; I only know the price God has required of me. God demands all. The decisive battle is nearly always over some apparently trivial issue, but in the sight of God there is nothing trivial. Upon this one vital issue in your life may depend the outcome of the whole battle. Remember that surrender at consecration is an advanced stage and consequently is more difficult than surrender at conversion. It is easier to give up what we see to be morally wrong, than to give up what may be right in itself, but not God's will for us.

The act of yielding must be incorporated into a life of submission. Consecration is only the threshold into

187

the Spirit-filled life. The act leads to an attitude, and the daily attitude leads to a richer and fuller life in Christ as our capacity increases.

WHAT I YIELD, GOD ACCEPTS

The second important fact is that what I yield, God accepts. A firm belief in this fact is all important. I have now definitely presented my body a living sacrifice to the Holy Spirit according to the exhortation of Romans 12:1. However, until I am sure in my heart, by faith, that God has accepted my offering, I can go no further. I can only continue to cry, "I surrender, I surrender." There are many who long to be filled and are willing for anything that will bring glory to God in their lives, who are frustrated and even in despair, because they are not conscious of anything revolutionary having taken place. They continue to cry, "I long to belong wholly to the Lord! I long to be used by Him! I surrender all I am and have to Thee, dear Lord," but they never look up and exclaim by faith, "What I yield, God accepts! I thank Thee, Lord Jesus, for this fact!" Once the realisation of the fact of the acceptance of God is established in the mind and heart, the seeking soul begins to make progress.

Because of the fact that God accepts all that I yield to Him, I must be careful to count the cost before I yield anything for His acceptance. We must not trifle with the holy God. God always reckons as His own that which He has been solemnly invited to take, and does with it according to His good pleasure. If we seek to take back and appropriate for our own use that which has been given to God, we are guilty of embezzlement. The moment we take ourselves off God's altar, that moment we become backsliders. God not only accepts the full surrender of our lives, but all our possessions. We know of a sister who surrendered all she was and all she possessed to the Lord for His use and His glory. Included in her possessions was a little cottage with beautiful hardwood floors, of which she was very proud. The Lord chose to use this cottage which He had accepted for a prayer meeting for the village women. There was a struggle in the heart of His child, because of what it would mean to the floors! At first she covered the floors with newspapers and placed the chairs on them when the women came. But the Lord was displeased. Then she came to see that when she gave herself to the Lord, she gave her cottage, and when she gave the cottage, she gave the floors; all were His and for His glory. What a blessing this revelation brought to her life!

WHAT GOD ACCEPTS, HE FILLS

The third important fact is that what God accepts, He fills. Many believers are severely tested by Satan at this juncture, because they do not pass through a highly emotional experience of which others have testified. At this point the believer must rest on the naked promise of the Word of God: "If any man thirst, let him come unto me and drink. He that believeth on me, as the Scripture has said, out of his belly shall flow rivers of living water." Just as surely as He accepts what I yield to Him, He fills it! There is no stereotyped experience of being filled with the Spirit, just as there is no stereotyped case of conversion. It is true that the fundamental facts are there, just as they are in the new birth, but our emotional experiences are not all the same. I knew a young French evangelist whom God saved on a lone country road, and he was so happy that

he immediately climbed the highest tree he could see!
I know of others who could only weep quietly for joy
that Christ was now their Saviour. F. B. Meyer and
Charles Inwood have told us that nothing highly emotional took place when they were filled with the Spirit,
but a deep inner peace flooded their souls, testifying
that they were now filled according to the promise of
God.

What I have yielded, God has accepted, and what
He has accepted He has filled for a purpose. We are
filled to do the will of God, whatever that may cost us.
Sometimes the will of God may lead us contrary to our
own natural expectations. There is a wide-spread mis-
conception as to the nature of the power of the Spirit,
so that many are looking for something they will
probably never receive. It does not follow that when
I am filled with the Spirit I will become a Charles
Finney or a Catherine Booth. Many have been keenly
disappointed because they have not received a sudden
acquisition of power to do the work which God has
assigned to someone else. God only fills us so that we
may have power to do that which He has appointed
for us to do. It does not necessarily follow that now I
am filled, the Holy Spirit will call me into full-time
Christian service. The mother must stay in the kitchen,
the father must work in the office or the factory, and the
children must study in school. God may call me to be
a foreign missionary, but on the other hand, He may
ask me to remain at home, when I would go. It was so
in the case of my own mother. She desired to be a
foreign missionary, but God chose her to stay at home
and to pray mightily for the missionaries and to support
them with her meagre income, and at the same time to
nourish her children, who were later to become missionaries.

To one is given the power of effective utterance, to another the ministry of intercession; and to another the enduement for patient suffering. He sets the members in the body "as it hath pleased Him" and then imparts to each member the power to fulfil his own individual function. As we see in the gifts of the Spirit in I Corinthians 12, some of these gifts are for service away from the limelight. Nevertheless, the lesser member receives the same enduement to perform his function for the glory of God as does the more prominent member.

Oftentimes it is only as we follow the guidance of the Holy Spirit into the pathway of service that we may expect the anointing of power for our service. I remember when I was a "boy-preacher" that the Spirit called me to go to the resort of Blackpool, near Liverpool, in the North-west of England. At this time I carried Gospel text-boards over my shoulder and in my hand, while preaching in the open air. When I arrived at that large, crowded, seaside resort, I was physically exhausted, and felt that I was not able to accomplish the work He had given me to do. In my room I prayed fervently for more than an hour for a fresh anointing of the Spirit for power and strength, but I was not conscious of an answer. Puzzled and perplexed, I started out to walk with my texts, but I soon returned because of my own human weakness. My wooden text-boards were very heavy, and it was difficult to walk always off the pavement in the busy heavy traffic, as I was required to do when carrying the text-boards. Besides all this, there were the insults and jeers of the ungodly, and the loneliness in my own heart, as a stranger in a large city. Again I prayed, crying to God earnestly for renewing, but again, although I had a sweet sense of the Father's presence, there was no con-

191

scious sense of great power for the task. In my confusion and desperation, I knew only one thing, and that was that God had called me for this week-end ministry in this specific city; that He had a work for me to do, and that I had to reach so many people for Christ in that city. On the strength of this assurance, I went forth without any feelings, unafraid, believing that as I went God would in some way meet my desperate need. Hallelujah! To my great joy, as I proceeded on my pathway of obedience, I was suddenly "anointed with fresh oil." All my doubts and fears were gone. Not only did I receive supernatural strength to preach many times and walk for hours each day, but also I received supernatural power, so that as I walked silently through the busy streets "holding forth the Word of life," I felt the mighty power of the living God resting upon me. It was hard for me to restrain myself from shouting "glory". Satan was defeated, and the Lord had given the victory.

Many believers today sit in their cosy armchairs by a comfortable fire, waiting until they are baptized with power, when the Lord wants them to go forth in faith, relying on Him!

WHAT GOD FILLS, HE USES

The fourth important fact is, what God fills, He uses. God is sure to lead you into service the moment your life is filled with Him. It is one thing to work for God; it is another thing to have God work through us. Your attitude of absolute surrender gives God the chance to work His perfect will through you. The moment you were saved, God had a perfect plan for your life. (Ephes. 2:10). The tragedy of the hour is that very few believers are living their lives in the center of the sweet, beloved will of God. They have planned their own lives. Occasionally, when in trouble, they cry to God for help. But the Spirit-filled believer has the joy of living the life that has been planned for him by the Father, and of knowing His enabling constantly. You now begin to co-operate in partnership with the Holy Spirit. God now wants to use you. And God will use you, but it will be in His own way and in His own time. As a foreign missionary, I believe that no child of God can really fulfil God's purpose for his life, unless he has a vision and an agony, not only for his next-door neighbour, but also for the heathen who lie in spiritual darkness.

> He was not willing that any should perish;
> Jesus, enthroned in the glory above,
> Saw our poor fallen world, pitied our sorrow,
> Poured out His life for us, wonderful love.
> Perishing, perishing, thronging our pathway,
> Hearts break with burdens too heavy to bear;
> Jesus would save, but there's no one to tell them,
> No one to save them from sin and despair.

In conclusion, let me state that there is no once-and-for-all filling that ignores a daily renewing. We cannot go on living and working as if God has entrusted us with an inexhaustible spiritual capital, upon which we can draw indefinitely. We must abide in Christ moment by moment for the constant manifestation and maintenance of the fulness of the Spirit. "I am persuaded that I shall obtain the highest amount of present happiness," said Murray McCheyne, "by maintaining a conscience always washed in Christ's blood; by being filled with the Holy Spirit at all times, and by attaining the most entire likeness to Christ in mind, will and

193

heart, that it is possible for a redeemed sinner to attain in this world."

Thy sovereign right, Thy gracious claim,
    To every thought and every power;
Our lives—to glorify Thy name,
    We yield Thee in this sacred hour.

Fill every chamber of the soul;
    Fill all our thoughts, our passions fill;
Till under Thy supreme control
    Submissive rests our cheerful will.

'Tis done; Thou dost this moment come;
    My longing soul is all Thine own;
My heart is Thy abiding home;
    Henceforth I live for Thee alone.

The altar sanctifies the gift;
    The blood insures the boon divine;
My outstretched hands to heaven I lift,
    And claim the Father's promise mine.

Now rise, exulting rise, my soul,
    Triumphant sing the Saviour's praise;
His name through earth and skies extol
    With all thy power through all thy days.

F. Bottome

I TAKE THE PROMISED HOLY GHOST
I TAKE THE GIFT OF PENTECOST
TO FILL ME TO THE UTTERMOST
I TAKE—*HE* UNDERTAKES

Name ....

Date ....